NOSH FOR ONE

BY JOY MAY

& the family team

THE NOSH FAMILY

We are the NOSH Family. We are a mum, a dad and two sons, working together in our family home. We've created recipes, cooked, eaten, photographed, designed and self-published this book, just for you. We want to remove the roadblocks to cooking for yourself and inspire you to get into the kitchen and create.

CONTENTS

LETTER FROM JOY

I set about writing this book after being inspired to help a number of family friends, who for one reason or another, prepare meals for one. The challenge can often be getting the inspiration or motivation to cook, rather than opting for ready-made meals, or making the same thing over and over again.

It is tempting to get normal recipes and just divide them by four in the hope that it works for one. But, as I am sure you know, that isn't always a success! Certain things just don't divide down (have you ever tried to quarter an egg!?), or you just end up with lots of leftover ingredients destined for the bin. I have had to, instead, re-think the approach to cooking, and even to shopping — but I will get into that later.

This really is a book for one; no bulk-cooking and filling your freezer with boxes of the same meal to be reheated later. Each recipe is designed as a stand-alone meal for one. On the occasion where there might be leftover ingredients, I have created 'paired recipes' to avoid any waste.

I hope that you will enjoy this book and find that it genuinely helps you in cooking for yourself and staying healthy.

Enjoy cooking.

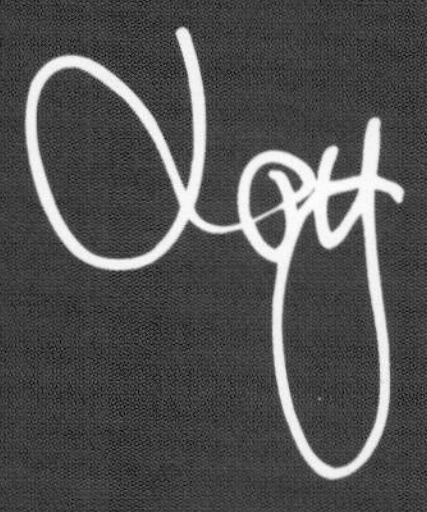

OUR ETHOS

THIS BOOK IS FOR YOU...

You might be part of the 8 million people in the UK who live by themselves, or the countless other people who, at the very least, simply 'cook for one'. For example:

- You might have launched out by yourself into a new career and have moved to a new city.
- You might live in a shared house with others, but you still cook for one.
- You might be a parent who eats at a different time and, maybe, wants to eat different food to your kids' choices.
- You might be at the other end of the scale and find yourself cooking for one again, after a long gap.

Whoever you are, we have had you in our minds while writing this book. There is a real range of scenarios you might find yourselves in, but here are the things we have tried to stick to throughout this book — perfect for one, right for you.

WHAT WE DON'T DO...

1. Divide meals for 4 by 4 and just hope that it works out for you.
2. Ignore the fact that your kitchen might not look like the average kitchen with lots of storage and freezer space.
3. Make you buy large packets of ingredients, causing you to waste what's left.

WHAT WE DO DO...

1. Design unique recipes just for you.
2. Make sure every recipe can be cooked with minimum space and utensils (see next page).
3. Choose ingredients where you can either buy exactly what you need, or point you to a 'paired recipe' where you can use up any leftovers you might have.

INGREDIENTS

Ingredient choice has been key for us with this book. Eliminating food waste has been at the front of our minds.

PRE-PACKED

We have chosen ingredients where you aren't forced to buy large packets, only to throw most of it away at the end of the week. In particular, we have chosen ingredients that are available at food counters in supermarkets, where you can buy just what you need. Even better, why not use the opportunity to visit your local butcher, or deli, and treat yourself to local ingredients and avoid unnecessary packaging at the same time?

STOCK

We specify 'liquid stock' for the first time in our books, to avoid having to crumble up stock cubes and only use a little bit at a time. The bonus is that liquid stock also tastes a lot better than stock cubes.

TINNED FOOD

We have avoided many tinned items that are only available in large sizes. We have used tinned items like coconut milk and tinned tuna, but only where smaller, single portion sizes are available. A lot of frozen items just take up too much room in what might be a small freezer. These have been avoided.

INGREDIENTS IN JARS

We have utilised some ingredients in jars like 'ready-roasted red peppers'. Here you can use what you need and store the rest in a way that preserves it well, rather than wasting a 'fresh' one.

VEGETABLES

When it comes to vegetables, we have sought to avoid using 'portions' of large veg. For example, with onions, we have specified using whole, 'small' onions or, where practical, opting for spring onions — you can just grab what you need and keep the rest of the bunch for another day.

HERBS

We love to use 'fresh herbs' in our recipes. However, they often come in a minimum pack of 25g, so, unless you eat the same herb for a week, there will be some wastage. We have two suggestions to get over this problem: one, is to buy a pot of herbs and keep them alive on your kitchen windowsill, in good light and kept watered. The other suggestion is to use frozen, fresh herbs, that work well and are better than dried herbs.

SUGAR!

Throughout this book you will see that we rarely use granulated sugar, white or brown, both of these are heavily processed forms of sweetness. Rather, we have mainly used honey or maple syrup.

In the case of honey, we would recommend RAW honey, that has not been pasteurised, or heavily filtered, thus, it doesn't lose its amazing resource of nutrients and enzymes. We get ours from local beekeepers, so that we also get the benefits of greater protection against seasonal allergies.

Generally, any maple syrup purchased is not heavily processed, but we would still recommend buying PURE maple syrup.

FREEZING RAW INGREDIENTS

If you do find yourself with more ingredients than you need, and you don't have any plans to cook with them in the next few days, there is a very simple way to freeze them. Simply cut any excess from the veg, slice things like beetroot into chunks, and cut broccoli into florets, etc.

Put each type of veg in a bowl and blanch with boiling water. Leave for 1 minute and drain. Plunge into very cold water and leave for 1 minute. Drain again and place in a freezer bag and pop into the freezer. Defrost when you want to use it.

You can freeze lemons and limes by simply cutting into 1/4's, placing in a freezer bag and popping into the freezer.

To freeze tofu, simply cut into cubes, place in a freezer bag, spread the cubes out in the bag and place in the freezer. Allow to defrost before using.

Some recipes call for small amounts of double cream. If you buy a 300ml carton, then simply pour the excess cream into freezer bags in small quantities, ready for other recipes. Place in the freezer, but leave plenty of time to defrost naturally.

EQUIPMENT

In our quest to keep things simple we have sought to use, in this book, as few utensils as possible, just in case you have a small kitchen, with limited space.

Opposite, is a picture of all that you need for cooking.

Throughout the photo shoots, to prepare this book, we never used more that two burners on the hob at the same time. This demonstrates that all the recipes are nice and simple, without having to juggle various pots and pans at the same time.

We cooked, using only a small casserole dish (approx. 14cm diameter), an ovenproof 20cm frying pan with a lid, a small saucepan with a lid, two baking trays and a ramekin. The only exception to the above was when we used a larger frying pan on p176, for one of our 'four-in-one' meals, but that was it — promise!

In our recipe photos, we have shown a few options for casserole dishes you might want to use, but, in reality, you only need one that can go under the grill, or into the oven.

Oh, and obviously we used our trusty mug (see next page)!

What is quicker than grabbing a mug and filling it? What is easier to remember than a mug of this, or 2 mugs of that!

This book is designed so that you don't need to use weighing scales. We have included the grams and ml measures for those who prefer a bit more precision, but, generally, these recipes don't require 'super-accurate' measurements to taste great.

Our mug holds 1/2 pint, or 300ml, of liquid and is the exact size of the mug pictured opposite. So find a mug that measures the same as this one and you won't go far wrong.

This actual mug is the same one I used when writing my first book back in 2000. It has a place in my heart. It has been broken and glued back together many times and has a special spot in our mug cupboard!

OUR MUG

ACTUAL SIZE
(300ML OR ½ PINT)

YOUR FREE NOSH BOOKS APP

To help you plan and shop for your food, we have designed a free app to create menus and shopping lists. Simply browse any of our books and add recipes of your choice to a weekly menu. The app does all the tedious work of creating the shopping list for you and boom! You are ready to shop.

No more aimless wandering around the supermarket, only to get home and still not be able to make a meal. What have you got to lose? Download it for FREE.

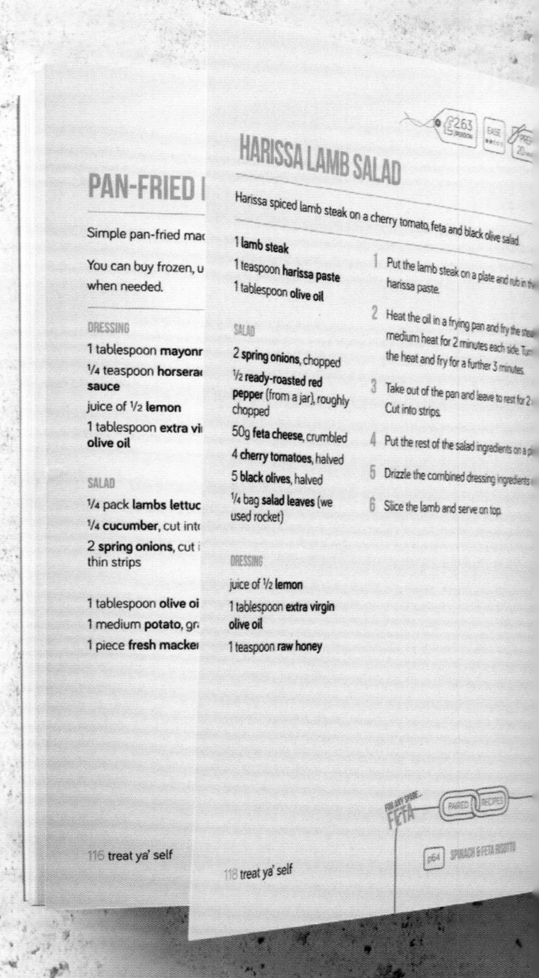

NOSH
FOR ONE
UNIQUE MEALS
JUST FOR YOU!
FREE
NOSH MENU
& SHOPPING
APP

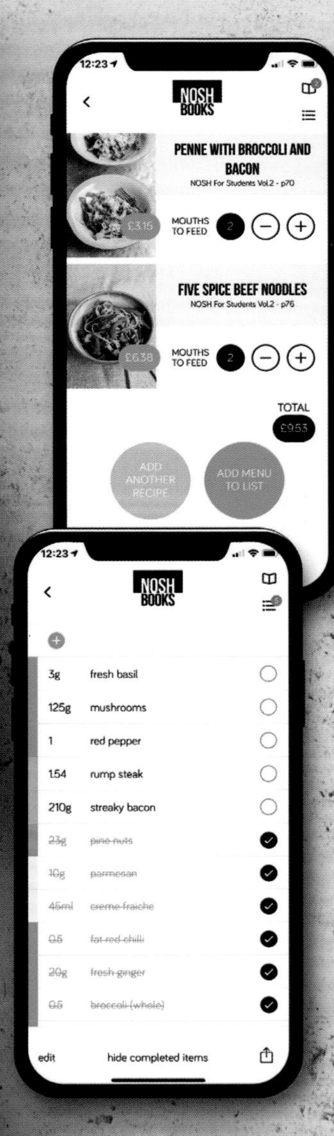
NOSH BOOKS
PENNE WITH BROCCOLI AND BACON
NOSH For Students Vol.2 - p70
MOUTHS TO FEED
FIVE SPICE BEEF NOODLES
NOSH For Students Vol.2 - p76
MOUTHS TO FEED
TOTAL
£9.53
ADD ANOTHER RECIPE
ADD MENU TO LIST
NOSH BOOKS
3g fresh basil
125g mushrooms
1 red pepper
1.54 rump steak
210g streaky bacon
23g pine nuts
10g parmesan
45ml creme fraiche
0.5 fat red chilli
20g fresh ginger
0.5 broccoli (whole)
edit
hide completed items

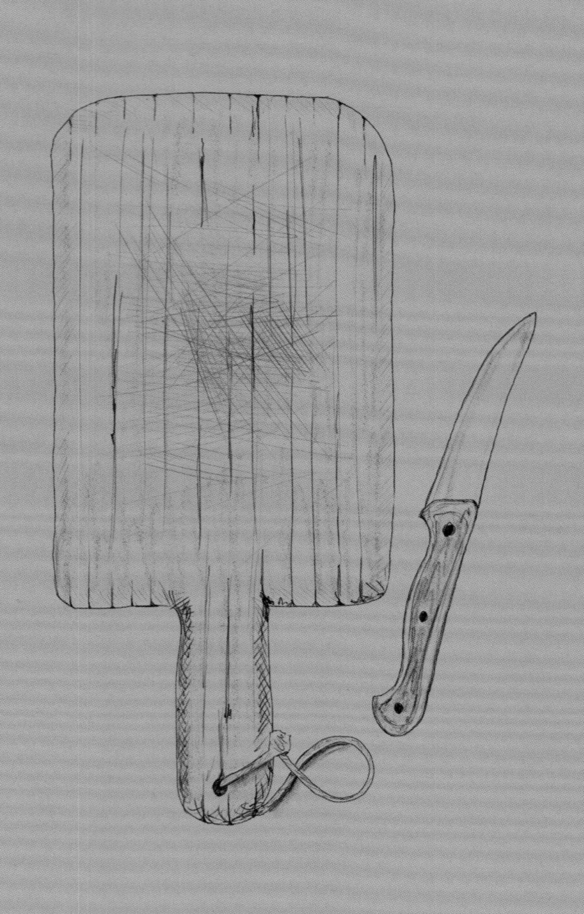

SNACKS

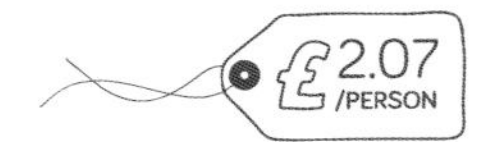

SMOKED SALMON & AVOCADO ON TOAST

Crushed avocado on seeded bread toast, topped with smoked salmon.

Smoked salmon usually comes in 100g packs. Use the rest in a sandwich with cream cheese and cucumber. You can also try one of our paired recipes below.

1/2 x 100g packet **smoked salmon trimmings**

2 **spring onions**, chopped

juice of 1/4 **lemon**

1 tablespoon **extra virgin olive oil**

1 slice **seeded bread**

1/2 **avocado**, peeled and squished

1/2 **Little Gem lettuce**

GLUTEN-FREE OPTION: use GF bread.

1. Put the salmon, onions, lemon and olive oil in a small bowl and mix. Season with salt and pepper and leave to stand for 10 minutes.
2. Toast the bread and spread the avocado on top.
3. Put the lettuce on top and then the salmon mix.

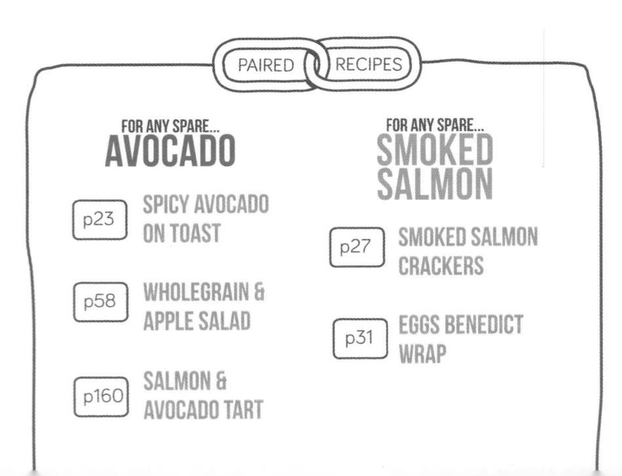

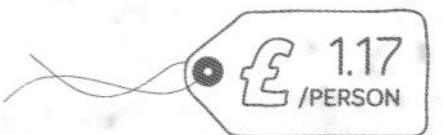

SARDINES ON TOAST

Sardines may seem a little old-fashioned. They are a good oily fish, however, high in Omega 3 and taste delicious to boot.

1 slice **bread**
1 **tomato**, sliced
95g tin **sardines**
juice of 1/4 **lemon**
1 teaspoon freshly chopped **basil**

GLUTEN-FREE OPTION: use GF bread.

1. Toast and butter the bread.
2. Arrange the tomatoes on the toast with the sardines on top. Squeeze over the lemon and sprinkle the basil on top.

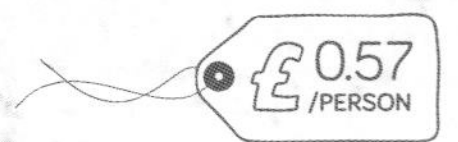

SPICY AVOCADO ON TOAST

Simple, spicy, crushed avocado on toast, topped with a poached egg. Works well for breakfast too.

1 slice **bread**

1/2 **avocado**, peeled and squished

1/4 **fat red chilli**, chopped

juice of 1/4 **lemon**

1 **egg**

GLUTEN-FREE OPTION: use GF bread.

1. Toast and butter the bread.
2. Mix together the avocado, chilli and lemon and spread on the toast.
3. Fill a frying pan with boiling, salted water. Carefully break a fresh egg into gently simmering water. Leave until the egg is set.
4. Put the poached egg on top. Season with salt and pepper.

PRAWN MAYO & ANCHOVIES ON TOAST

Try to vary the breads you use for toast; try not to use just white bread. Also, buy anchovies in jars, as they are easy to store in the fridge.

1 slice **bread**
1 mug (100g) defrosted **frozen prawns**
2 tablespoons **mayo**
juice of 1/4 **lemon**
3 **anchovies** from a jar

GLUTEN-FREE OPTION: use GF bread.

1. Toast and butter the bread.
2. Mix together the prawns, mayo and lemon. Pile onto the toast, with the anchovies on top.

ALMOND BUTTER & BANANA ON TOAST

We make a bit of a habit of putting bananas in sandwiches. We realise it's a bit bizarre, but give it a try.

1 slice **bread**

2 tablespoons **almond butter**

1 **banana**, sliced

1 teaspoon **sesame seeds**

1 teaspoon **honey**

GLUTEN-FREE OPTION: use GF bread.

1. Toast and butter the bread.
2. Spread the almond butter on the toast.
3. Add the sliced banana. Sprinkle over the sesame seeds and then drizzle with the honey.

CRACKER SNACKS

There seems something indulgent about piling lovely ingredients high onto a cracker.

Vary the crackers you use. A packet will keep better than bread, if you store it in an airtight box.

For all of the following recipes, butter before adding the ingredients and use 2 crackers per serving.

GLUTEN-FREE OPTION: use GF crackers, or oat biscuits.

TUNA & MAYO

110g tin **tuna**, drained

2 tablespoons **mayo**

1/2 teaspoon **Dijon mustard**

2 **spring onions**, chopped

EGG & MAYO

1 **egg**, hard-boiled and chopped

1 tablespoon **mayo**

1 **pickled gherkin**, chopped

SMOKED SALMON

1/2 x 100g pack **smoked salmon trimmings**

2 tablespoons **cream cheese**

1/8 **cucumber**, chopped

PATÉ & CHUTNEY

85g **chicken liver pate**

2 tablespoons **mango chutney**

GOATS' CHEESE & OLIVES

100g **goats' cheese**, sliced

1 tablespoon **sweet chilli sauce**

6 **black olives**, halved

BACON & TOMATO

2 tablespoons **garlic and herbs cream cheese**

4 rashers **bacon**, fried and sliced

3 **cherry tomatoes**, halved

BL DOUBLE T WRAP

Just so you know the second 'T' is for the Tabasco. A game changing addition!

2 teaspoons **olive oil**
3 rashers **bacon**
1 tablespoon **mayo**
1 **tortilla**
1/2 **Little Gem lettuce**
1/2 **avocado**, sliced
1 **tomato**, sliced
1/4 teaspoon **Tabasco sauce**

GLUTEN-FREE OPTION:
use GF tortilla.

1. Heat the oil in a frying pan and fry the bacon until crisp.
2. Spread the mayo on the tortilla.
3. Add the lettuce, avocado, tomato and bacon.
4. Drizzle over the Tabasco and roll up the tortilla.

PAIRED RECIPES

FOR ANY SPARE...
AVOCADO

p23 SPICY AVOCADO ON TOAST

p58 WHOLEGRAIN & APPLE SALAD

FOR ANY SPARE...
BACON

p27 BACON & TOMATO CRACKER

p66 CHICKEN & BACON WITH APPLE SLAW

CHICKEN & PEANUT BUTTER WRAP

Pan-fried chicken breast with a satay-style sauce. Perfect for a protein boost as well.

2 teaspoons **olive oil**
1 **chicken breast**
1 tablespoon **peanut butter**
1 teaspoon **soy sauce**
1 teaspoon **honey**
1 teaspoon **water**
1 **tortilla**
1/2 **Little Gem lettuce**
1 **spring onion**, sliced

GLUTEN-FREE OPTION: use GF tortilla and soy sauce.

1. Heat the oil in a frying pan and fry the chicken, on a high heat, for 2 minutes each side. Then fry on a low heat, with a lid on the pan, for 4 minutes each side. If you have a small piece of chicken, reduce the last stage to 3 minutes each side. Leave to rest for 2 minutes, then slice.
2. Mix together the peanut butter, soy, honey and water.
3. Spread on the tortilla. Add the lettuce, sliced chicken and spring onions and roll up.

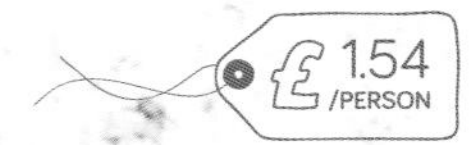

TUNA & PICKLE WRAP

This tuna and pickled cucumber combo, with a kick of cayenne, is a real winner.

110g tin **tuna**, drained

2 tablespoons **mayo**

1/2 teaspoon **cayenne pepper**

1/2 **Little Gem lettuce**

1 **tortilla**

1 piece **pickled cucumber**, sliced

2 **spring onions**, finely chopped

GLUTEN-FREE OPTION: use GF tortilla.

1 Mix together the tuna, mayo and cayenne pepper.

2 Put the lettuce on the tortilla and add the tuna mix, together with the pickled cucumbers and onions.

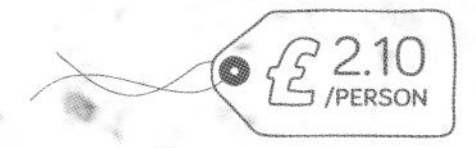

EGGS BENEDICT WRAP

Scrambled eggs with smoked salmon and a mustard and caper mayonnaise.

10g **butter**
2 **eggs**, beaten
1/4 teaspoon **Dijon mustard**
2 tablespoons **mayo**
1 teaspoon **capers**
1 **tortilla**
1/2 **Little Gem lettuce**
1 **spring onion**, finely chopped
50g **smoked salmon**

GLUTEN-FREE OPTION: use GF tortilla.

1. Melt the butter in a frying pan and add the beaten eggs. Season with salt and pepper and scramble the eggs. Keep them quite soft.
2. Mix together the mustard, mayo and capers and spread on the tortilla.
3. Add the lettuce, spring onions, and smoked salmon. Finally, add the scrambled eggs and roll up the wrap.

ROSTI WITH MACKEREL & PISTACHIO FETA

Flaked mackerel on a crunchy, potato rosti, topped with pistachio feta.

1 tablespoon **olive oil**
1 medium **potato**, grated
25g **pistachios**
25g **feta cheese**
1 tablespoon **olive oil**
1 tablespoon **Greek yogurt**
zest of 1/4 **lemon**
1/2 x 200g packet **smoked mackerel**
watercress or **salad leaves**
1/8 **cucumber**, diced
juice of 1/4 **lemon**

1. Heat the oil in a frying pan. Season the grated potato with salt and pepper and add loosely into the pan. Fry on a medium heat until golden brown on both sides.
2. Meanwhile, blitz the pistachios with a hand-held blender until quite small. Add the feta, oil, yogurt and lemon zest. Blitz again.
3. Skin and flake the mackerel.
4. Serve everything together with a squeeze of lemon juice over the top.

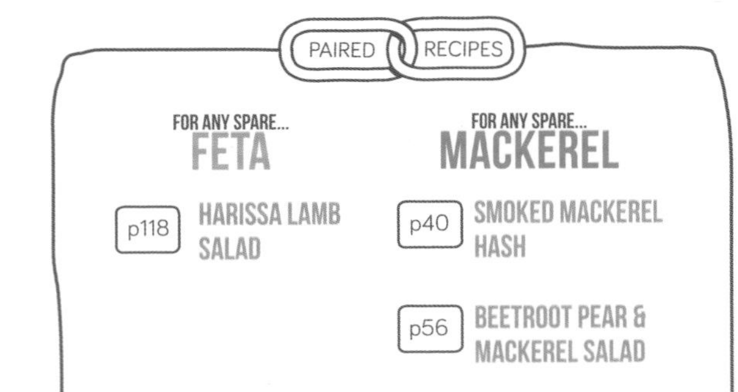

PAK CHOI & BRIE OMELETTE

Folded omelette filled with melted Brie and topped with mushrooms and pak choi.

The Brie inside the omelette goes 'super-gooey' and delicious.

10g **butter**
2 **eggs**, beaten
100g **Brie**, sliced
1 tablespoon **toasted sesame oil**
75g **mushrooms**, sliced
1 **pak choi**, sliced
2 teaspoons **soy sauce**
2 teaspoons **honey**

GLUTEN-FREE OPTION: use GF soy sauce.

1. Heat the butter in a frying pan. Season the egg with salt and pepper. Add to the pan and allow to spread. Fry until browned lightly underneath. Turn over, add the Brie on top and continue to fry the omelette until browned.
2. Fold the omelette over and place on the plate. Set to one side until needed.
3. Heat the oil in the frying pan. Add the mushrooms and fry, on a high heat, for 1 minute. Add the pak choi, soy and honey and fry, on a high heat, for 1 minute.
4. Serve on the omelette.

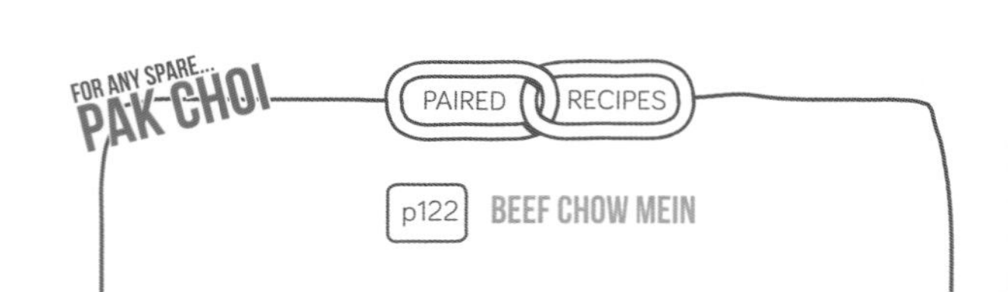

p122 BEEF CHOW MEIN

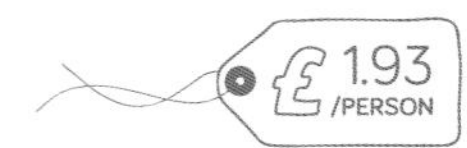

ASPARAGUS & NOODLE OMELETTE

A different take on an omelette. Here, with added noodles that go nice and crunchy when you fry them. Fried asparagus is just the best too!

50g **dried rice noodles**

1 tablespoon **toasted sesame oil**

125g **asparagus**

1/2 **fat red chilli**

1 clove **garlic**, sliced

2 teaspoons freshly grated **ginger**

1/2 **ready-roasted red pepper** (from a jar), chopped

2 **eggs**, beaten

1. Put the noodles in a bowl and cover with boiling water. Leave to stand for 10 minutes and then drain.
2. Meanwhile, heat the oil in a frying pan. Fry the asparagus until it is nicely browned. Take out of the pan and set to one side.
3. Add the chilli and garlic to the pan and fry until the garlic browns a little. Add the ginger and fry for 30 seconds.
4. Add the pepper and drained noodles to the pan and spread them out evenly.
5. Season the egg with salt and pepper and pour into the pan. Once the omelette is lightly browned on the bottom, turn over and brown on the other side.
6. Serve with the asparagus on top.

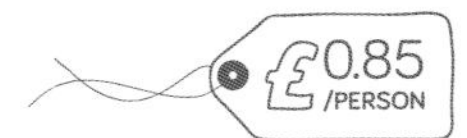

TUNA ROSTI & FRIZZLED EGG

Tuna and potato rosti topped with a fried egg and crushed peas. Rosti is a great way to cook potatoes quickly. It also adds lots of flavour.

1 medium **potato**, grated
60g tin **tuna**, drained
1 tablespoon **olive oil**
1 **egg**
3/4 mug (100g) defrosted **frozen peas**
10g **butter**

1. Mix together the grated potato and tuna. Season with salt and pepper.
2. Heat the oil in a frying pan. Pile the mixture into the pan and spread out a little. Fry on a medium heat for 3–4 minutes. Carefully turn over and fry on the other side.
3. Take out of the pan and set aside on a plate.
4. Break the egg into the pan and fry on a high heat, allow it to frizzle around the edges.
5. Put the peas in a saucepan of boiling water and simmer for 1 minute.
6. Drain, return to the pan, and mash along with the butter. Serve.

SMOKED MACKEREL HASH

You might guess we are partial to a bit of fish! Ready-cooked smoked mackerel served with a potato hash and soft-boiled egg.

1 medium **potato**, cut into small chunks

1 **egg**

1 tablespoon **olive oil**

2 **spring onions**, chopped

½ x 160g pack **smoked mackerel**

DRESSING

1 tablespoon freshly chopped **basil**

1 tablespoon **extra virgin olive oil**

juice of ¼ **lemon**

1. Put the potatoes in a saucepan of boiling, salted water and simmer for 5 minutes. Add the egg (in its shell) and simmer for a further 5 minutes. Drain the potatoes and egg. Return the potatoes to the pan and set the egg to one side.
2. Heat the oil in a frying pan. Add the spring onions and potatoes and season well with salt and pepper. Fry until the potatoes are browned.
3. Flake the mackerel into the pan and stir. Transfer to a plate.
4. Gently peel the egg and serve on top.
5. Drizzle over the combined dressing ingredients.

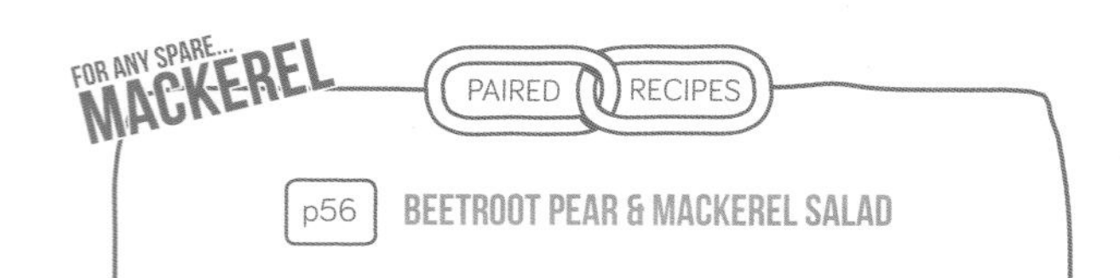

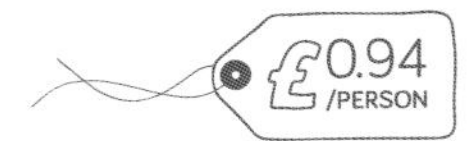

CROQUE A LA NOSH

This is such a simple way to elevate the humble sandwich into something incredible. If you fry things slowly, the cheese in the middle should be nice and melted (although I think Tim was in a hurry the day we photographed this one, as the cheese hasn't melted that much. It still tasted amazing.)

2 slices **bread**, buttered

2 slices **ham**

1/2 mug (40g) grated **Cheddar cheese**

1 teaspoon **Dijon mustard**

1 **egg**, beaten

1 tablespoon **olive oil**

GLUTEN-FREE OPTION: use GF bread.

1. Make up the sandwich with the bread, ham and cheese, spreading the mustard on one of the slices of bread.
2. Put the beaten egg on a plate, season with salt and pepper, and dip the sandwich in it, allowing the egg to soak into the bread.
3. Heat the oil in a frying pan and gently fry the sandwich on both sides.

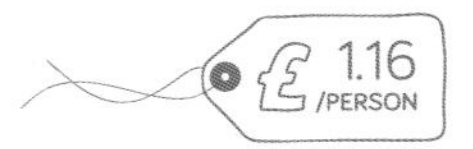

BACON & EGG HASH

Bacon, onion and potato, fried in coconut oil, topped with a thinly sliced omelette.

1 medium **potato**, cut into chunks

2 tablespoons **coconut oil**

4 rashers **streaky bacon**

1 small **red onion**, sliced

1 **egg**, beaten

1 Put the potato in a saucepan of boiling, salted water and simmer for 8 minutes. Drain.

2 Put half of the coconut oil in a frying pan, add the bacon, and fry until crispy. Remove from the pan and cut into bite-sized chunks.

3 Add the onion and drained potatoes to the pan and fry gently until everything begins to brown. Add the bacon back to the pan, season with pepper, and stir together. Turn out onto the plate.

4 Add the rest of the oil to the pan and fry the beaten egg. Flip over and fry the other side. Remove from the pan and cut into strips.

5 Serve on top of the hash.

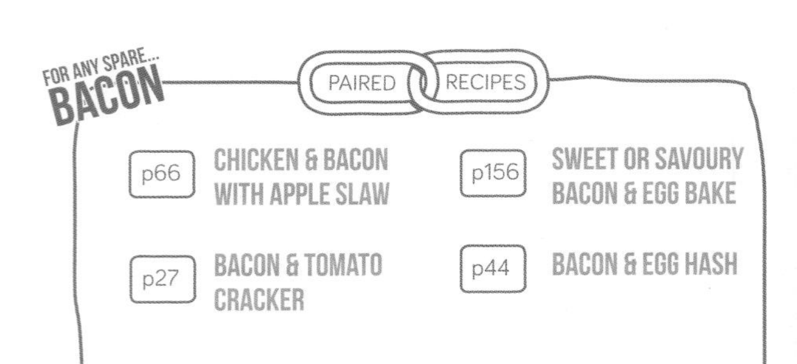

p66 CHICKEN & BACON WITH APPLE SLAW
p156 SWEET OR SAVOURY BACON & EGG BAKE
p27 BACON & TOMATO CRACKER
p44 BACON & EGG HASH

SUPER FAST

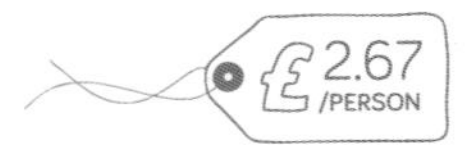

SALMON & SESAME NOODLES

Seared salmon fillet on sesame and spinach noodles.

50g **dried rice noodles**

1 tablespoon **toasted sesame oil**

1 fillet **salmon**

1 teaspoon **sesame seeds**

50g **fresh spinach**

1 tablespoon **soy sauce**

1 teaspoon **honey**

GLUTEN-FREE OPTION: use GF soy sauce.

1. Put the noodles in a bowl and cover with boiling water. Leave to stand for 10 minutes and then drain.
2. Meanwhile, heat the oil in a frying pan and fry the salmon, skin side down at first, until nicely browned. Then turn over the salmon and fry until lightly browned and cooked through. Remove from the pan and set to one side.
3. Add the sesame seeds to the pan along with the spinach. Heat until the spinach wilts.
4. Add the drained noodles, soy and honey to the pan and mix together.
5. Serve the salmon on top of the noodle mix.

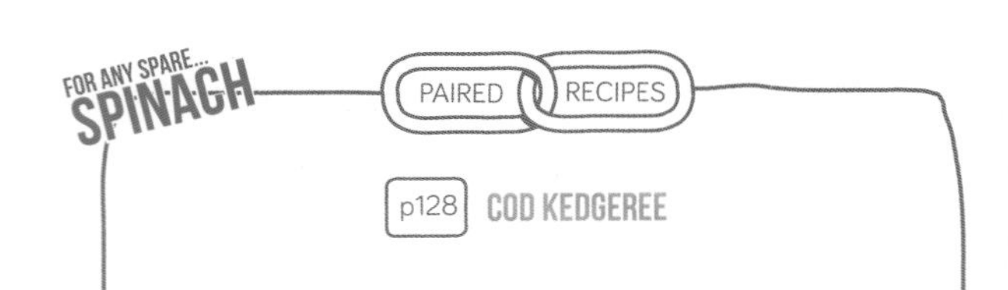

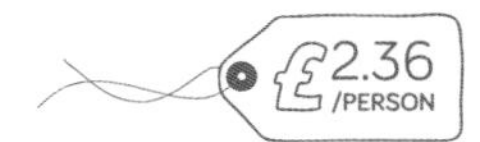

SATAY CHICKEN NOODLES

Chicken and chilli noodles with a peanut satay sauce and crunchy mangetout.

50g **dried rice noodles**

¼ mug (40g) **unsalted peanuts**

2 teaspoons **toasted sesame oil**

2 **spring onions**, chopped

1 clove **garlic**, chopped

½ **fat red chilli**, chopped

1 **chicken breast**, cut into chunks

50g **mangetout**

SAUCE

¼ mug (75ml) **water**

1 tablespoon good quality **peanut butter**

2 teaspoons freshly grated **ginger**

1 tablespoon **tahini paste**

2 teaspoons **honey**

VEGETARIAN OPTION: use 100g Quorn chicken-style pieces.

1. Put the noodles in a bowl and cover with boiling water. Leave to stand for 10 minutes and then drain.
2. Meanwhile, heat the frying pan and dry-fry the peanuts until they begin to brown a little. Remove from the pan.
3. Add the oil to the pan and fry the onion, garlic and chilli for 1 minute.
4. Add the chicken and fry until it is browned.
5. Add the mangetout and peanuts. Season with salt and pepper.
6. Mix together the sauce ingredients and add to the pan. Bring to the boil.
7. Add the drained noodles and stir in.

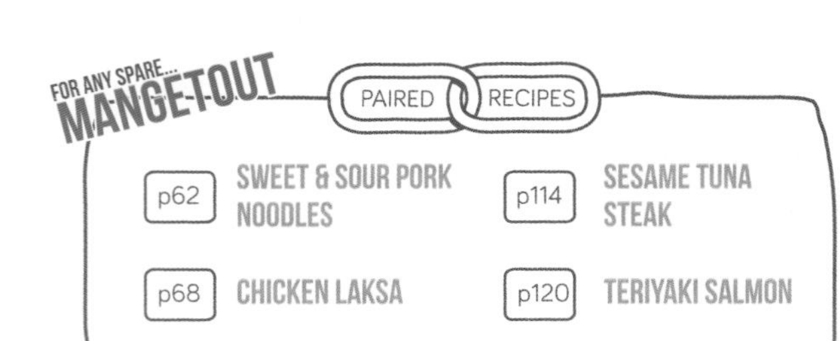

p62 SWEET & SOUR PORK NOODLES
p114 SESAME TUNA STEAK
p68 CHICKEN LAKSA
p120 TERIYAKI SALMON

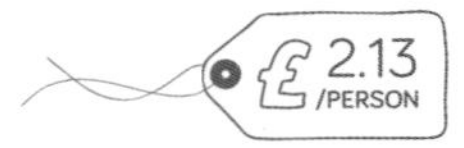

GF OPTION V OPTION

CHICKEN & PECAN PASTA

Simple pasta dish with chicken and pecans with a creamy mustard and crème fraîche sauce.

1/2 mug (35g) **pasta** (we used penne)

1 tablespoon **olive oil**

1 **chicken breast**, cut into bite-sized pieces

75g **mushrooms**, sliced

1/4 mug (20g) **pecan nuts**, roughly chopped

2 **spring onions**, chopped

100g **crème fraîche**

1 teaspoon **Dijon mustard**

1 tablespoon freshly chopped **basil**

GLUTEN-FREE OPTION: use GF pasta.

VEGETARIAN OPTION: use 100g Quorn chicken-style pieces.

1. Put the pasta in a saucepan of boiling, salted water. Simmer until tender, drain and return to the pan.
2. Meanwhile, heat the oil in a frying pan. Add the chicken and fry until no longer pink on the outside.
3. Add the mushrooms and fry for 2–3 minutes.
4. Add the pecans, onions, crème fraîche and mustard. Cook for 2–3 minutes.
5. Add the pasta and the basil.

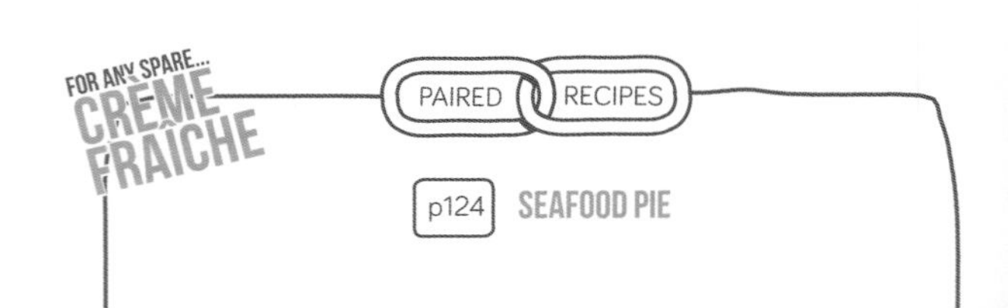

THAI POACHED SALMON

This is a lovely one-pot dish in which, while the rice is cooking, the salmon is poached on top. This can be a spicy dish, or not-so-spicy, depending on the curry paste you use.

1 fillet **salmon**
1 teaspoon **soy sauce**
1 teaspoon **honey**
2 teaspoons **toasted sesame oil**
3 **spring onions**, chopped
1/3 mug (80g) **basmati rice**
165ml tin **coconut milk**
1/2 mug (150ml) **water**
1 tablespoon **Thai red curry paste**

rocket or **salad leaves**

DRESSING

juice of 1/4 **lemon**
1 teaspoon **honey**
1 tablespoon **extra virgin olive oil**

GLUTEN-FREE OPTION: use GF soy sauce and curry paste.

1. Put the salmon steak in a bowl with the soy sauce and honey. Leave to stand until needed.
2. Meanwhile, heat the oil in a frying pan, add the onions and rice, and fry for 1 minute. Add the coconut milk, water and curry paste. Season with salt and pepper and bring to the boil.
3. Add the salmon to the pan and continue to simmer gently, with a lid on the pan, for 10 minutes.
4. Serve with the salad, drizzled with the combined dressing ingredients.

BEETROOT PEAR & MACKEREL SALAD

Flaked mackerel on grated raw beetroot and sliced pear salad.

DRESSING

1 tablespoon **extra virgin olive oil**

1 tablespoon **cider vinegar**

2 teaspoons **honey**

½ **Little Gem lettuce**

1 **raw beetroot**, grated

½ small **red onion**, thinly sliced

1 **carrot**, peeled and grated

120g **smoked mackerel**, flaked

1 **pear**, cored and sliced

1 tablespoon **sesame seeds**

1. Mix together the dressing ingredients and season with salt and pepper.
2. Arrange the lettuce on the plate.
3. Mix together the beetroot, onion and carrot. Put on top of the lettuce.
4. Add the mackerel and pear. Sprinkle the sesame seeds on top and drizzle the dressing over.

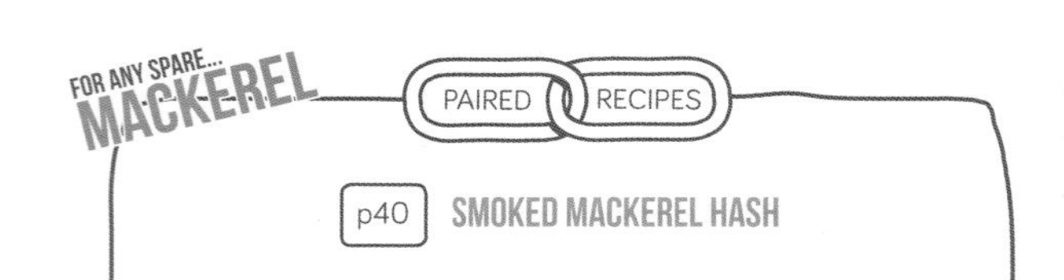

p40 SMOKED MACKEREL HASH

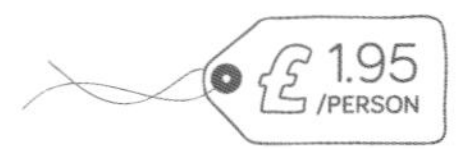

WHOLEGRAIN & APPLE SALAD

Super-easy, using pre-cooked, mixed wholegrain rice with a smoked paprika sauce.

You can use the rest of the wholegrain rice mixture in other salads. We used Tilda brown rice, quinoa and wild rice in this photo.

1/2 x 220g pack **cooked, mixed wholegrain rice**

1/2 **pink lady apple**, cored and chopped

3 **ready-to-eat dried apricots**, chopped

2 **spring onions**, chopped

1/2 **avocado**, chopped

juice of 1/4 **lemon**

1 **Little Gem lettuce**

DRESSING

1 tablespoon **mayo**

1 tablespoon **extra virgin olive oil**

juice of 1/4 **lemon**

1/4 teaspoon **smoked paprika**

1. Mix together the wholegrain rice, apple, apricots, spring onions, avocado and lemon juice.
2. Arrange the lettuce leaves on the plate. Add the wholegrain mixture.
3. Mix together the dressing ingredients and drizzle over.

p160 'NO-PASTRY' SALMON & AVOCADO TART

p23 SPICY AVOCADO ON TOAST

GOATS' CHEESE & SPINACH FRITTATA

'One-pot' potato and egg frittata with melted goats' cheese. Fry everything and then stick it under the grill to brown.

1 tablespoon **olive oil**

1 medium **potato**, cut into chunks

1 small **red onion**, chopped

1 clove **garlic**, chopped

100g **spinach**

2 **eggs**, beaten

1 tablespoon freshly chopped **basil**

50g **goats' cheese**, sliced

1/4 bag **salad leaves** (we used babyleaf and rocket)

1. Preheat the grill.
2. Heat the oil in a frying pan, add the potatoes and fry, with a lid on the pan, until they begin to brown. Add the onion and garlic and fry until everything browns.
3. Add the spinach and fry for 1 minute.
4. Beat together the egg and basil and add to the pan. Allow the eggs to set on the bottom of the pan and then gently stir once to allow unset egg to reach the base of the pan.
5. Place the goats' cheese on top and place under the grill until nicely browned.
6. Serve with the salad.

p27 GOATS' CHEESE & OLIVE CRACKERS

SWEET & SOUR PORK NOODLES

Sliced pork steak, mangetout and baby sweetcorn in a maple syrup and soy sauce.

50g **dried rice noodles**

1 tablespoon **toasted sesame oil**

1 **pork steak**, sliced

2 **spring onions**, chopped

½ x 200g pack **baby sweetcorn and mangetout**, sliced lengthways

SAUCE

¼ mug (75ml) **water**

1 teaspoon **cornflour**

2 teaspoons **tomato purée**

2 tablespoons **cider vinegar**

2 tablespoons **maple syrup**

2 teaspoons **soy sauce**

GLUTEN-FREE OPTION: use GF soy sauce.

1. Put the noodles in a bowl and cover with boiling water. Leave to stand for 10 minutes and then drain.
2. Meanwhile, heat the oil in a frying pan and add the sliced pork. Season well with salt and pepper and fry until nicely browned on both sides.
3. Add the onions, sweetcorn and mangetout and fry for 1 minute.
4. Mix together the sauce ingredients and add to the pan. Bring to the boil and simmer until the sauce begins to thicken.
5. Mix in the drained noodles and serve.

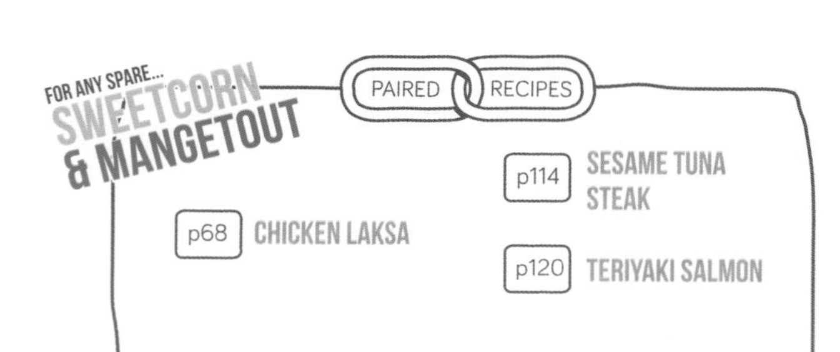

SPINACH & FETA RISOTTO

'One-pot' basmati risotto with fresh spinach and pine nuts.

1 tablespoon **olive oil**
1 small **red onion**, chopped
1 clove **garlic**, chopped
1/3 mug (80g) **basmati rice**
2/3 mug (200ml) **water**
1 teaspoon **liquid veg stock**
50g **fresh spinach**
juice of 1/4 **lemon**
1/4 mug (15g) grated **Parmesan cheese**
2 tablespoons (20g) **pine nuts**
50g **feta**, crumbled

GLUTEN-FREE OPTION: use GF stock.

VEGETARIAN OPTION: use Parmesan-style cheese.

1. Heat the oil in a frying pan. Add the onions and garlic and fry for 2 minutes, or until the garlic begins to brown.
2. Add the rice and fry for 1 minute.
3. Add the water and stock and bring to the boil. Simmer gently, with a lid on the pan, for 10 minutes. Remove from the heat.
4. Add the spinach and mix through. Keep stirring gently until the spinach wilts.
5. Stir in the lemon juice, Parmesan and pine nuts and heat through for 30 seconds.
6. Serve with the feta crumbled over the top.

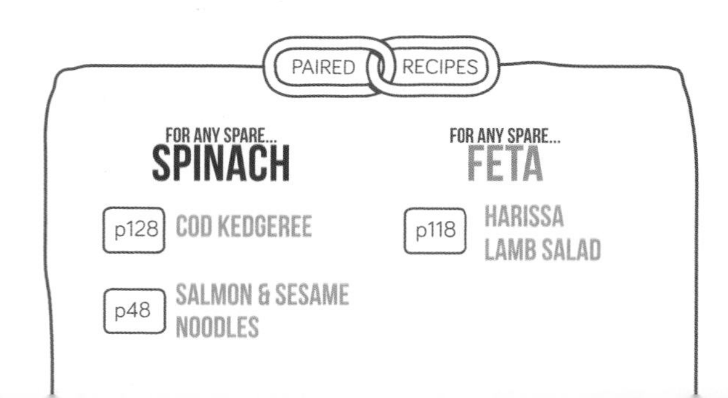

CHICKEN & BACON WITH APPLE SLAW

Pan-fried chicken breast on a rough apple slaw, topped with crunchy bacon bits.

1 tablespoon **olive oil**

1 **chicken breast**

4 rashers **streaky bacon**

APPLE SLAW

1/2 **Little Gem lettuce**, sliced

1/2 **apple**, cut into sticks

1 **spring onion**, chopped

2 tablespoons **mayo**

1/2 teaspoon **honey**

1 tablespoon **cider vinegar**

1 tablespoon **pine nuts**

1. Heat the oil in a frying pan and add the chicken breast and bacon. Fry the chicken, on a high heat, for 2 minutes each side. Fry the bacon until crisp and remove. Continue frying the chicken, on a low heat, with a lid on the pan, for a further 4 minutes each side.
2. Meanwhile, mix together the slaw ingredients.
3. Chop the bacon into bite-sized pieces.
4. Slice the chicken and serve on top of the slaw with the bacon.

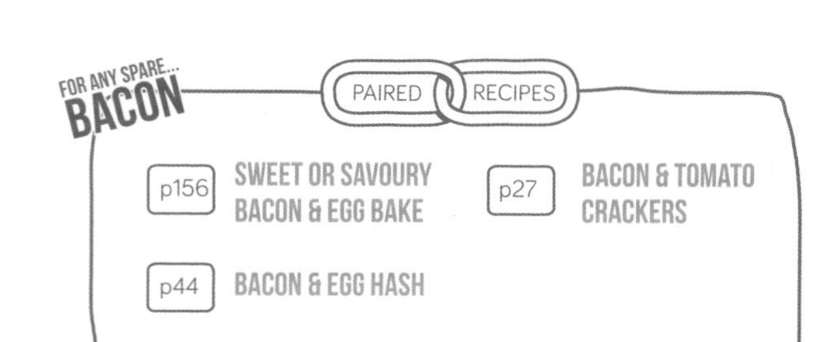

p156 SWEET OR SAVOURY BACON & EGG BAKE
p27 BACON & TOMATO CRACKERS
p44 BACON & EGG HASH

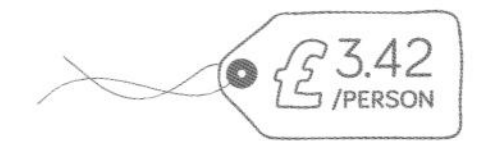

CHICKEN LAKSA

Chicken noodles in a lightly spiced Thai broth, with baby sweetcorn and mangetout.

1 tablespoon **toasted sesame oil**

1 tablespoon freshly grated **ginger**

1 clove **garlic**, chopped

½ **fat red chilli**, chopped

zest of ¼ **lemon**

165ml tin **coconut milk**

1 teaspoon **liquid chicken stock**

2 teaspoons **fish sauce**

1 **chicken breast**, cut into bite-sized pieces

½ x 200g pack **mangetout and sweetcorn**, halved lengthways

150g **fresh egg noodles**

GLUTEN-FREE OPTION: use GF stock and rice noodles instead of egg noodles.

1. Heat the oil in a frying pan. Add the ginger, garlic and chilli. Fry for 30 seconds.
2. Add the lemon zest, coconut milk, liquid stock and fish sauce.
3. Bring to the boil and add the chicken. Simmer for 3–4 minutes. Check that the chicken is cooked through.
4. Add the sweetcorn and mangetout and simmer for 1 minute.
5. Stir in the egg noodles and simmer for 1 minute. If you use dried egg noodles, you will need to cook them first before adding to the laksa.

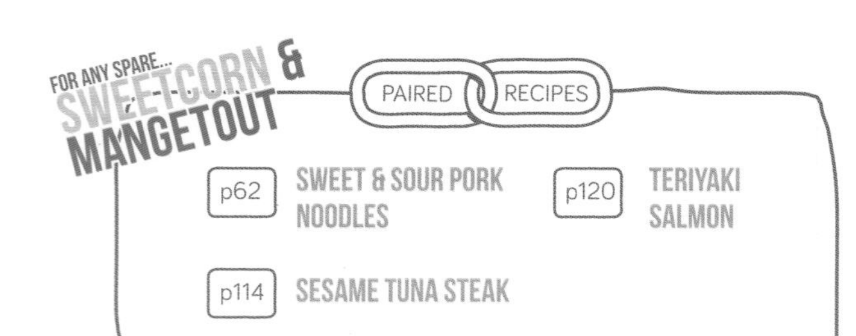

PARMA HAM & PESTO RISOTTO

Green pesto risotto with edamame beans, Parma ham and goats' cheese.

Use any spare Parma in a wrap with some lettuce, pickled cucumbers and tomatoes.

Use the spare goats' cheese on toast with either some smoked salmon trimmings or some sweet chilli sauce.

10g **butter**
2 **spring onions**, chopped
1/3 mug (80g) **basmati rice**
2/3 mug (200ml) **water**
1 teaspoon **liquid veg stock**
1/2 mug (75g) defrosted **frozen edamame beans**
1 tablespoon **green pesto**
75g **soft goats' cheese**
40g **Parma ham**

GLUTEN-FREE OPTION: use GF stock.

1. Heat the butter in frying pan. Add the spring onions and fry for 30 seconds.
2. Add the rice and allow it to absorb the butter. Add the water, stock and edamame beans. Simmer gently, with a lid on the pan, for 10 minutes.
3. Stir in the pesto and heat for 1 minute. Season with salt and pepper.
4. Serve with blobs of the goats' cheese and the Parma ham.

B
B
A
A
C
C

IT HAS TO BE EASY

COCONUT PRAWN RISOTTO

'One-pot' Korma prawn risotto with ready-roasted red peppers.

1 teaspoon **coconut oil**

2 **spring onions**, chopped

1/3 mug (80g) **basmati rice**

165ml tin **coconut milk**

1/3 mug (100ml) **water**

2 teaspoons **Korma curry paste**

100g defrosted **cooked, frozen prawns**

1/2 **ready-roasted red pepper** (from a jar), chopped

1. Heat the coconut oil in a frying pan. Add the spring onions and fry for 1 minute.
2. Add the rice and allow it to absorb the juices from the pan.
3. Add the coconut milk, water and curry paste and bring to the boil. Season well with salt and pepper.
4. Simmer gently, with a lid on the pan, for 10 minutes.
5. Add the prawns and red peppers and simmer for 1 minute.

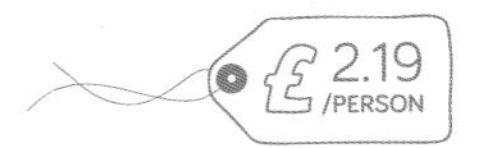

GRILLED HAM HOCK PASTA

A cheat's pasta and ham hock bake, with wholegrain mustard and Gruyère cheese, that just goes under the grill.

1/2 mug (50g) **pasta** (we used fusilli)

90g **ham hock**, pulled apart

2 **spring onions**, chopped

3 tablespoons (45ml) **soured cream**

1 tablespoon **sundried tomato purée**

2 teaspoons **wholegrain mustard**

1/4 mug (20g) grated **Gruyère cheese**

GF OPTION: use GF pasta.

1. Put the pasta in a saucepan of boiling, salted water. Simmer for 8 minutes, or until cooked. Drain, retaining 2 tablespoons of the cooking liquid, and return to the pan.
2. Preheat the grill.
3. Mix the ham hock, spring onions, soured cream, tomato purée and mustard in a small bowl and add to the drained pasta, along with the 2 tablespoons of retained cooking liquid. Mix and heat through for 1 minute.
4. Pour into a small casserole dish and sprinkle over the grated cheese.
5. Grill until nicely browned.

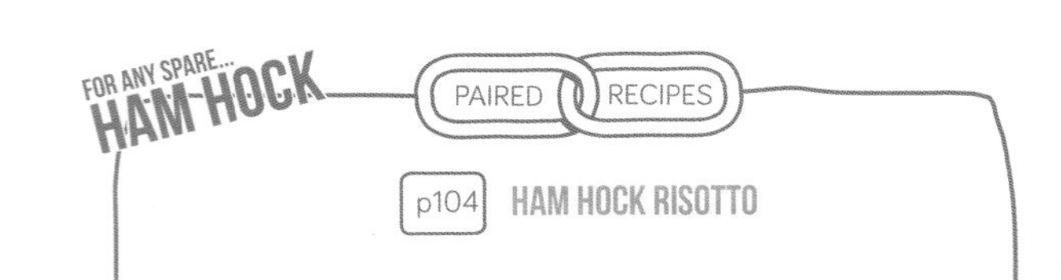

p104 HAM HOCK RISOTTO

LE CREUSET

TUNA PASTA WITH ANCHOVIES & CAPERS

Fusilli pasta with tuna and cherry tomatoes, topped with anchovies and capers. A good dish to use up some store cupboard items.

2/3 mug (65g) **pasta** (we used fusilli)

1 tablespoon **olive oil**

1 small **red onion**, chopped

2 teaspoons **capers**

4 **cherry tomatoes**, halved

110g tin **tuna**, drained and flaked

1 tablespoon freshly chopped **basil**

3 **anchovies**, sliced lengthways

GLUTEN-FREE OPTION: use GF pasta.

1. Put the pasta in a saucepan of boiling, salted water. Simmer for 8 minutes. Drain and return to the pan.
2. Heat the oil in a frying pan and fry the onions and capers for 3–4 minutes.
3. Add the tomatoes and fry for 1 minute.
4. Mix in the tuna and basil and drained pasta.
5. Serve with anchovies on top

FRENCH ONION SOUP

Simple French onion soup with Cheddar cheese croutons.

10g **butter**

1 tablespoon **olive oil**

1 **onion**, sliced

1 clove **garlic**, chopped

1 teaspoon **liquid beef stock**

1 mug (300ml) **water**

1 slice **seeded bread**

5g **butter**

1/4 mug (20g) grated **Cheddar cheese**

GLUTEN-FREE OPTION: use GF stock and bread.

VEGETARIAN OPTION: use veg stock.

1. Heat the butter and oil in a frying pan and fry the onion and garlic on a medium heat until nicely browned.
2. Preheat the grill.
3. Add the stock and water. Bring to the boil and simmer for 2 minutes.
4. Meanwhile, toast the bread and spread with the butter, sprinkle over the cheese and place under the grill until the cheese bubbles. Cut into croutons and serve on top of the soup.

COD & VEGETABLE BAKE

Quick to prepare. Whack it in the oven and then, at the end, just grill the cod on top.

1 medium **potato**, cut into chunks

5 **cherry tomatoes**

1 small **red onion**, sliced

10 **green olives**

1/4 teaspoon **mixed dried herbs**

1/4 mug (75ml) **boiling water**

1 teaspoon **liquid veg stock**

1 teaspoon **olive oil**

cod fillet

zest of 1/4 **lemon**

1 teaspoon **olive oil**

GLUTEN-FREE OPTION: use GF stock.

1. Preheat the oven to 180°C fan/200°C/gas 6.
2. Grease a small casserole dish and put in the potatoes, tomatoes, onions, olives and herbs. Mix the stock and water together and add. Season with salt and pepper and mix all together. Drizzle one teaspoon of olive oil over the top.
3. Place in the oven for 40 minutes.
4. Preheat the grill. Take the casserole out of the oven and place the fish on top. Sprinkle with the lemon zest. Season with salt and pepper and drizzle with the other teaspoon of olive oil. Grill for 5-6 minutes until the fish browns lightly.

SIMPLE COTTAGE PIE

Simple beef mince flavoured with balsamic vinegar and topped with potato.

1 medium **potato**, cut into chunks

1 tablespoon **olive oil**

1 small **red onion**, chopped

125g **minced beef**

1 teaspoon **flour**

2 teaspoons **balsamic vinegar**

½ teaspoon **honey**

1 teaspoon **liquid beef stock**

¼ mug (75ml) **water**

1 tablespoon **olive oil**

GLUTEN-FREE OPTION: use GF stock and flour.

VEGETARIAN OPTION: use Quorn mince and veg stock.

1. Preheat the oven to 180°C fan/200°C/gas 6.
2. Put the potato in a saucepan of boiling, salted water and simmer for 6 minutes. Drain and return to the pan.
3. Meanwhile, heat the oil in a frying pan and add the onion. Fry until it begins to soften.
4. Add the mince and fry until no longer pink.
5. Add the flour and mix well. Add the balsamic, honey, stock and water and bring to the boil. Simmer until the sauce thickens. Place in a small casserole dish.
6. Arrange the potatoes on the top, season with salt and pepper and drizzle with the olive oil. Bake in the oven for 35 minutes.

SMOKED PAPRIKA & COCONUT CHICKEN

Smoked paprika chicken, poached in coconut milk and served with pea rice.

1 **chicken breast**
1 teaspoon **smoked paprika**
1 tablespoon **olive oil**
2 **spring onions**, chopped
1 teaspoon freshly grated **ginger**
1 clove **garlic**, chopped
165ml tin **coconut milk**
1/3 mug (80g) **basmati rice**
2/3 mug (200ml) **water**
1/2 mug (75g) defrosted **frozen peas**

1. Put the chicken breast on a plate and add the paprika. Rub into the chicken evenly.
2. Heat the oil in a frying pan and fry the chicken for 2 minutes each side.
3. Add the spring onions, ginger and garlic to the pan and fry for 1 minute. Season well with salt and pepper.
4. Add the coconut milk and simmer gently, with a lid on the pan for 10 minutes.
5. Meanwhile, put the rice in a saucepan with the water. Simmer gently, with a lid on the pan, for 8 minutes. Add the peas and simmer for a further 2 minutes. Stir the peas into the rice.
6. Slice the chicken after cooking and serve with the rice.

SPICED POACHED CHICKEN

Poaching chicken is not only an easy, healthy way to cook, but it also produces the most tender and tasty chicken out there!

1 **chicken breast**

1/3 mug (80g) **basmati rice**

1/2 teaspoon **turmeric**

1/2 teaspoon **ground cumin**

1/2 teaspoon **ground coriander**

1 tablespoon **raisins**

1 tablespoon **cashew nuts**, roughly chopped

2 **spring onions**, chopped

1 **ready-roasted red pepper** (from a jar), chopped

1 tablespoon freshly chopped **basil**

DRESSING

2 tablespoons **mayo**

juice of 1/2 a **lemon**

2 teaspoons **honey**

1. Put the chicken in a saucepan of boiling, salted water. Bring to the boil, then take off the heat and leave to stand, with a lid on the pan, for 15 minutes. Once cooked, remove from the pan and slice.
2. Meanwhile, put the rice in a saucepan with 2/3 mug boiling water and the turmeric, cumin and coriander. Simmer gently, with a lid on the pan, for 10 minutes.
3. Add the raisins, cashews, spring onions, peppers and basil to the rice. Season well and mix.
4. Serve the chicken on the rice and drizzle with the combined dressing ingredients.

CHILLI BEEF BAKE

This can be cooked in one pan, if you have a frying pan that can go in the oven.

1 tablespoon **olive oil**
1 small **red onion**, chopped
1 clove **garlic**, chopped
125g **minced beef**
1 **tomato**, chopped
1/2 teaspoon **dried basil**
2 teaspoons **tomato purée**
1 teaspoon **Worcestershire sauce**
1 pinch **dried chilli flakes**
1/3 mug (80g) **basmati rice**
1 teaspoon **liquid beef stock**
2/3 mugs (200ml) **water**
1/2 mug (40g) grated **Cheddar cheese**

GLUTEN-FREE OPTION: use GF stock and GF soy sauce instead of Worcestershire Sauce.

VEGETARIAN OPTION: use quorn mince, soy sauce instead of Worcestershire, and vegetable stock cube.

1. Preheat the oven to 180°C fan/200°C/gas 6.
2. Heat the oil in a frying pan. Add the onions and garlic and fry until the onions soften.
3. Add the mince and fry until no longer pink.
4. Add the rest of the ingredients, apart from the cheese. Mix together and bring to the boil.
5. If your frying pan is ovenproof, no need to transfer. Otherwise, pour into a small casserole dish, top with the grated cheese and bake in the oven for 25 minutes.

POACHED CHICKEN & MUSTARD POTATOES

Lovely fresh dish. Poaching chicken retains so much flavour and keeps it tender.

1 **chicken breast**

150g **new potatoes**, chopped

1/2 mug (75g) defrosted **frozen peas**

2 tablespoons **mayo**

1 teaspoon **Dijon mustard**

1 **pickled cucumber**, chopped

2 **spring onions**, chopped

1. Put the chicken breast in a saucepan of boiling, salted water. Bring back to the boil, take off the heat, and leave to rest, with a lid on the pan, for 15 minutes. Take the chicken out of the pan and set to one side until needed.

2. Put the potatoes in a saucepan of boiling, salted water. Simmer for 9 minutes, add the peas, and simmer for 1 minute. Drain.

3. Mix together the mayo, mustard, pickled cucumber, spring onions and sliced chicken and combine with the potatoes and peas.

PANCETTA RISOTTO

Crispy fried, pancetta lardon risotto with peas and Parmesan. Make sure you give the onions and pancetta time to brown nicely as this really adds to the flavour.

1 teaspoon **olive oil**
1 small **red onion**, sliced
1 clove **garlic**, chopped
60g pack **pancetta lardons**
1/3 mug (70g) **risotto rice**
1/2 teaspoon **dried basil**
2/3 mug (200ml) **water**
1 teaspoon **liquid chicken stock**
1/2 mug (75g) defrosted **frozen peas**
1/4 mug (15g) grated **Parmesan cheese**
juice of 1/4 **lemon**

GLUTEN-FREE OPTION: use GF stock.

1. Heat the oil in a frying pan. Add the onion, garlic and pancetta and fry until nicely browned.
2. Add the rice to the pan and cook for 30 seconds, allowing it to absorb the juices from the pan.
3. Add the basil, water and stock and bring to the boil. Season with salt and pepper. Turn down to simmer gently, with a lid on the pan, for 10 minutes, until the rice is tender.
4. Stir in the peas and Parmesan and allow to warm through for 1 minute.
5. Add the lemon juice and mix.

CHILLI CHICKEN PENNE

Chicken and pasta with juicy cherry tomatoes and shavings of Parmesan.

2/3 mug (45g) **pasta** (we used penne)

2 teaspoons **olive oil**

2 **spring onions**, chopped

1/4 **fat red chilli**, chopped

1 clove **garlic**, chopped

1 **chicken breast**, cut into bite-sized pieces

100g **cherry tomatoes**, halved

1/2 tablespoon freshly chopped **basil**

Parmesan cheese shavings

GLUTEN-FREE OPTION: use GF pasta.

VEGETARIAN OPTION: use 100g Quorn chicken-style pieces and Parmesan-style cheese.

1. Put the pasta in a saucepan of boiling, salted water and simmer for 10 minutes. Drain and return to the pan.
2. Meanwhile, heat the oil in a frying pan and add the onions, chilli and garlic. Fry for 1 minute.
3. Add the chicken and fry until it is no longer pink.
4. Add the cherry tomatoes and fry for 3–4 minutes until the tomatoes soften and begin to fall apart.
5. Add the basil and cooked pasta and mix. Serve with some Parmesan shavings on top.

SALMON FRITTATA

Quick and easy way to make a complete meal in one small pan. Potatoes and salmon with a melted Parmesan topping.

1 tablespoon **toasted sesame oil**

1 medium **potato**, cut into chunks

1 **spring onion**, chopped

1 fillet **salmon**, cut into bite-sized pieces

2 **eggs**, beaten

zest of 1/4 **lemon**

1/4 mug (15g) grated **Parmesan cheese**

1. Preheat the grill.
2. Heat the oil in a frying pan, add the potatoes and season with salt and pepper. Cook on a low heat, with a lid on the pan, for 5 minutes, or until the potatoes begin to brown and are tender. Stir frequently.
3. Add the spring onions and salmon and cook for 1 minute.
4. Add the egg and lemon zest, season with salt and pepper, and allow to cook on the bottom for 2 minutes.
5. Sprinkle over with the Parmesan cheese and place under the grill. The top should brown lightly and the egg set.

TUNA GRILL

When you thought a tuna bake couldn't get any easier. Voila, the 'Tuna Grill'!!

3/4 mug (75g) **pasta** (we used fusilli)

1 tablespoon **olive oil**

1 tablespoon **capers**

2 **spring onions**, chopped

1 clove **garlic**, chopped

75g **mushrooms**, sliced

6 **cherry tomatoes**, halved

110g tin **tuna**, drained

1/2 mug (40g) grated **Cheddar cheese**

GLUTEN-FREE OPTION: use GF pasta.

1. Put the pasta in a saucepan of boiling, salted water and simmer for 10 minutes. Drain and return to the pan.
2. Preheat the grill.
3. Heat the oil in a frying pan and add the capers, onions and garlic. Fry for 2 minutes.
4. Add the mushrooms and tomatoes and fry for another 2 minutes.
5. Add the tuna and pasta, season with salt and pepper and gently mix together.
6. Pour into a small casserole dish and pile the cheese on the top.
7. Place under the grill until the cheese begins to bubble and brown.

LE CREUSET

SWEET & SOUR TOFU

You can freeze any leftover Tofu. Simply cut into chunks and freeze, see p10.

1/3 mug (80g) **basmati rice**

1 tablespoon **toasted sesame oil**

1/2 x 280g block **firm tofu**, cut into bite-sized chunks

1/2 **red apple**, cut into small chunks

2 **spring onions**, chopped

2 teaspoons freshly grated **ginger**

1 clove **garlic**, chopped

1/2 **ready-roasted pepper** (from a jar), chopped

SAUCE

75ml (1/4 mug) **apple juice**

1 teaspoon **mirin rice wine vinegar**

2 teaspoons **tomato purée**

1 teaspoon **honey**

1 teaspoon **cornflour**

1. Put the rice in a saucepan with 2/3 mug of boiling water. Simmer gently, with a lid on the pan, for 10 minutes. Remove from the heat.
2. Meanwhile, heat the oil in a frying pan, add the tofu, and season with salt and pepper. Fry until it begins to brown, add the apple and continue to fry until the tofu is nicely browned.
3. Add the spring onions, ginger and garlic and fry for 1 minute.
4. Add the pepper and fry for 30 seconds.
5. Mix together the sauce ingredients and add to the pan. Simmer for 1 minute. The sauce should thicken.
6. Serve with the rice.

HAM HOCK RISOTTO

Really good, one-pan recipe. If you have leftover Cambazola, it is great on toast, or crackers, with some good chutney. However, if you buy it from a cheese counter, you shouldn't need to have any leftovers.

10g **butter**

2 **spring onions**, sliced

1/3 mug (80g) **basmati rice**

2/3 mug (200ml) **water**

1 teaspoon **liquid chicken stock**

100g **ham hock**

1/2 mug (75g) defrosted **frozen peas**

1 tablespoon freshly chopped **basil**

85g **Cambazola blue cheese**, sliced

1/4 bag **salad leaves** (we used rocket)

GLUTEN-FREE OPTION: use GF stock.

1. Heat the butter in a frying pan, add the onions, and fry for 1 minute. Add the rice and fry for 1 minute. Season with salt and pepper.
2. Add the water and stock and bring to the boil. Simmer gently, with a lid on the pan, for 10 minutes.
3. Preheat the grill.
4. Stir the ham, peas and basil into the rice mixture.
5. Add the sliced cheese on top and place under the grill until the cheese browns lightly.
6. Serve with the rocket leaves (you don't have to throw them all over the table, Ben was just feeling 'arty' that day).

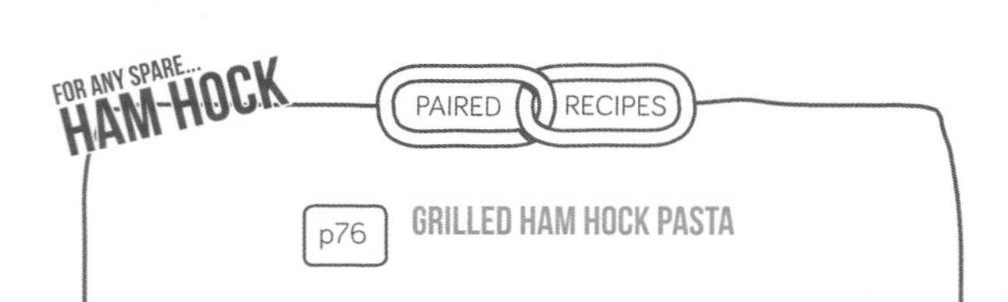

EASE ★★★☆☆

PAD THAI PRAWNS

Prawns with a medjool date and lime marinade topped with toasted peanuts.

MARINADE

2 **medjool dates**, finely chopped

2 tablespoons **water**

3 **anchovies**, finely chopped

juice of ½ **lime**

¼ **fat red chilli**, chopped

100g **cooked Jumbo prawns**

50g **dried rice noodles**

2 tablespoons **peanuts**

1 teaspoon **olive oil**

1 **egg**, beaten

1 teaspoon **olive oil**

2 **spring onions**, chopped

1 tablespoon freshly chopped **coriander**

1. Mix together the marinade ingredients. Add the prawns, mix and set to one side.
2. Put the noodles in a bowl and cover with boiling water. Leave to stand for 10 minutes and then drain.
3. Put the chopped peanuts in a dry frying pan and toast. Take out of the pan and set to one side.
4. Heat 1 teaspoon of olive oil in the pan, add the egg, and swish around to form a large, flat omelette. Once cooked, remove from the pan and slice.
5. Heat another teaspoon of olive oil in the frying pan and fry the prawns.
6. Add the spring onions to the pan and fry for 30 seconds.
7. Add half the coriander and the drained noodles and heat through.
8. Mix in the chopped egg and sprinkle over with the peanuts and the rest of the coriander.

DIJON SALMON BAKE

Creamy, salmon pasta bake, where everything is mixed together with cooked pasta and put under the grill.

1 mug (100g) **pasta** (we used fusilli)

3 **spring onions**, chopped

1 tablespoon freshly chopped **chives**

1/3 mug (100ml) **double cream**

1 teaspoon **capers**

1 teaspoon **Dijon mustard**

100g tin **salmon**, drained

1/3 mug (25g) grated **Cheddar cheese**

GLUTEN-FREE OPTION: use GF pasta.

1. Grease a small casserole dish.
2. Put the pasta in a saucepan of boiling, salted water, simmer for 10 minutes, and then drain.
3. Preheat the grill.
4. In a large bowl, mix together the pasta, spring onions, chives, cream, capers and mustard. Flake the salmon and gently mix in. Season with salt and pepper.
5. Pour into the casserole dish. Sprinkle the cheese over the top and grill until the cheese begins to brown.

LE CREUSET
LE CREUSET

TREAT YA SELF

STEAK & HORSERADISH ROASTIES

Rump steak with horseradish potatoes and a rich chilli and red onion gravy.

- 2 medium **potatoes**, cut into small chunks
- 1 tablespoon **olive oil**
- 2 teaspoons **horseradish sauce**
- 1 tablespoon **olive oil**
- 1 small **red onion**, sliced
- 1 clove **garlic**, chopped
- 1/4 **fat red chilli**, sliced
- 1 teaspoon **flour**
- 1/3 mug (100ml) **water**
- 1 teaspoon **red wine vinegar**
- 1/2 teaspoon **liquid beef stock**
- 1 tablespoon **olive oil**
- 1 **rump steak**

GLUTEN-FREE OPTION: use GF flour and stock.

1. Preheat the oven to 200°C fan/220°C/gas 7.
2. Put the potatoes in a bowl and add the olive oil and horseradish. Season with salt and pepper and mix everything together. Turn out onto a baking tray, spread out and roast in the oven for 40 minutes.
3. Meanwhile, put the other tablespoon of olive oil in a saucepan, and add the onions and garlic. Fry on a medium heat for 7–8 minutes until nicely caramelised. Season well with salt and pepper. Add the chilli and fry for 1 minute. Add the flour, mix together, and fry for 30 seconds. Add the water, wine vinegar and stock and simmer for 2 minutes. Set to one side.
4. Season the steak with salt and pepper and rub into both sides.
5. 10 minutes before the end of the cooking time for the potatoes, heat the olive oil in a frying pan and add the steak. Fry for 2 minutes each side on a high heat. Cook longer if you like your steak less rare.
6. Reheat sauce if needed and serve.

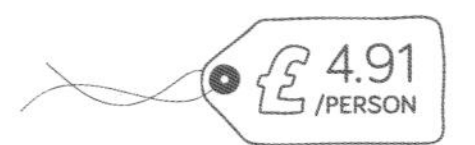

SESAME TUNA STEAK

Sesame seed covered tuna steaks with turmeric rice and a honey and lemon sauce.

1/3 mug (80g) **basmati rice**

1/4 teaspoon **turmeric**

1/2 x 200g pack **mangetout and sweetcorn**, halved lengthways

1 tablespoon **sesame seeds**

1 **tuna steak**

1 tablespoon **toasted sesame oil**

SAUCE

2 **spring onions**, chopped

4 teaspoons **soy sauce**

2 teaspoons **honey**

juice of 1/2 **lemon**

GLUTEN-FREE OPTION: use GF soy sauce.

1. Put the rice in a saucepan with 2/3 mug of boiling water and the turmeric. Simmer gently, with a lid on the pan, for 10 minutes. Take off the heat and add the mangetout and sweetcorn. Put the lid back on the pan and set to one side until needed.

2. Put the sesame seeds on a plate and press the tuna into them until coated.

3. Heat the oil in a frying pan and fry the tuna, on a medium heat, for 1 minute each side. It is good for the tuna to be pink in the middle. Remove from the pan.

4. To make the sauce, add the onions to the pan, and fry for 1 minute. Add the rest of the ingredients and bring to the boil.

5. Stir the mangetout and sweetcorn into the rice and serve with the tuna and the sauce.

p62 SWEET & SOUR PORK NOODLES
p120 TERIYAKI SALMON
p68 CHICKEN LAKSA

PAN-FRIED MACKEREL & ROSTI

Simple pan-fried mackerel on potato rosti, served with a horseradish dressing.

You can buy frozen, uncooked mackerel. Very handy to keep in the freezer and pull out when needed.

DRESSING

1 tablespoon **mayo**

1/4 teaspoon **horseradish sauce**

juice of 1/2 **lemon**

1 tablespoon **extra virgin olive oil**

SALAD

1/4 pack **lambs lettuce**

1/4 **cucumber**, cut into strips

2 **spring onions**, cut into thin strips

1 tablespoon **olive oil**

1 medium **potato**, grated

1 piece **fresh mackerel**

1. Mix together the dressing ingredients.
2. Mix the salad ingredients in a bowl. Add the dressing and mix.
3. Heat the oil in a frying pan and loosely place in the grated potato. Season with salt and pepper. Fry on each side for 3–4 minutes until golden brown. Take out of the pan and put on the plate.
4. Add the mackerel to the pan, season with salt and pepper and fry for about 1 minute on both sides until lightly browned. Serve on top of the rosti and with the salad.

HARISSA LAMB SALAD

Harissa spiced lamb steak on a cherry tomato, feta and black olive salad.

1 **lamb steak**

1 teaspoon **harissa paste**

1 tablespoon **olive oil**

SALAD

2 **spring onions**, chopped

1/2 **ready-roasted red pepper** (from a jar), roughly chopped

50g **feta cheese**, crumbled

4 **cherry tomatoes**, halved

5 **black olives**, halved

1/4 bag **salad leaves** (we used rocket)

DRESSING

juice of 1/2 **lemon**

1 tablespoon **extra virgin olive oil**

1 teaspoon **honey**

1. Put the lamb steak on a plate and rub in the harissa paste.
2. Heat the oil in a frying pan and fry the steak, on a medium heat, for 2 minutes each side. Turn down the heat and fry for a further 3 minutes.
3. Take out of the pan and leave to rest for 2 minutes.
4. Put the rest of the salad ingredients on a plate.
5. Drizzle over the combined dressing ingredients.
6. Slice the lamb and serve on top.

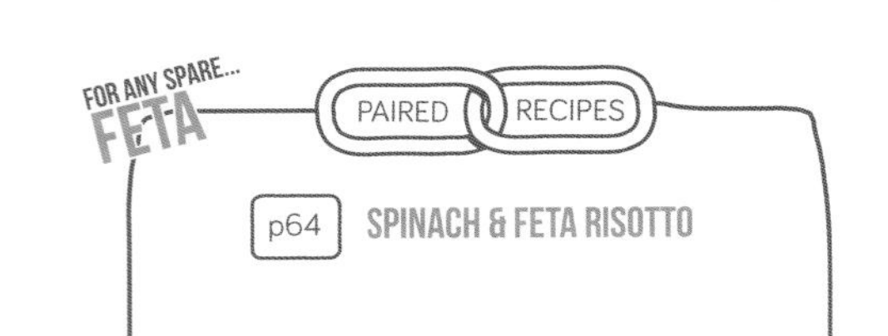

p64 SPINACH & FETA RISOTTO

TERIYAKI SALMON

Mirin marinated salmon fillet on rice noodles with sweetcorn and mangetout.

MARINADE

2 tablespoons **soy sauce**

2 teaspoons **honey**

2 tablespoons **mirin rice wine vinegar**

1 fillet **salmon**

50g **dried rice noodles**

1 tablespoon **olive oil**

1/2 x 200g pack **baby sweetcorn and mangetout**, sliced

1 tablespoon freshly chopped **coriander**

1 teaspoon **sesame seeds**

GLUTEN-FREE OPTION: use GF soy sauce.

1. Put the marinade ingredients in a small bowl along with the salmon and leave to stand for 10 minutes.
2. Meanwhile, put the noodles in a bowl and cover with boiling water. Leave to stand for 10 minutes and then drain.
3. Meanwhile, heat the oil in a frying pan and add the salmon. Keep the marinade for later. Gently fry on one side for 3 minutes.
4. Add the sweetcorn and mangetout to the pan. Turn over the salmon and cook for a further 2 minutes. Keep stirring the sweetcorn and mangetout.
5. Add the marinade to the pan and simmer for 1 minute.
6. Serve with the drained noodles, coriander and sesame seeds.

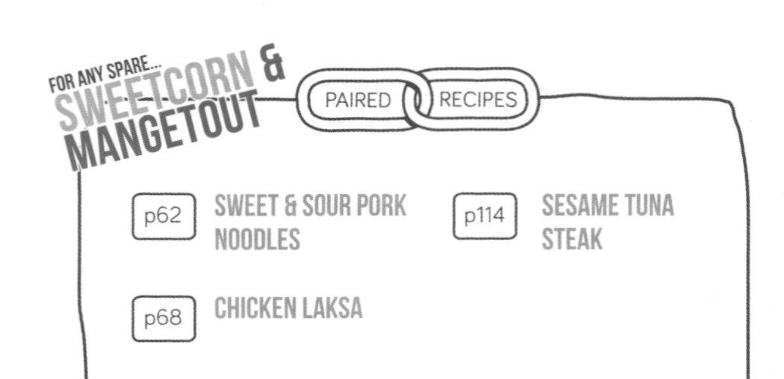

BEEF CHOW MEIN

Slices of rump steak in a mirin and honey sauce with chilli, pak choi and red peppers.

50g **dried rice noodles**

SAUCE

4 teaspoons **soy sauce**

1 tablespoon **mirin rice wine vinegar**

1 tablespoon **honey**

1 teaspoon **cornflour**

3 tablespoons **water**

1 tablespoon **toasted sesame oil**

1 **rump steak**, thinly sliced

2 **spring onions**, chopped

1 clove **garlic**, chopped

2 teaspoons freshly grated **ginger**

1/2 **fat red chilli**, chopped

1 **pak choi**, sliced

1 **ready-roasted red pepper** (from a jar), chopped

GLUTEN-FREE OPTION: use GF soy sauce.

1. Put the noodles in a bowl and cover with boiling water. Leave to stand for 10 minutes and then drain.
2. Meanwhile, mix together the sauce ingredients.
3. Heat the oil in a frying pan and add the steak. Fry on a high heat until browned. Remove from the pan and set to one side.
4. Add the onions, garlic, ginger and chilli to the pan and fry for 30 seconds. Add the pak choi to the pan and fry for 1 minute.
5. Add the peppers, sauce and steak to the pan and cook for 1 minute. The sauce should thicken.
6. Serve with the drained noodles.

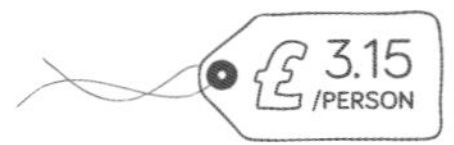

SEAFOOD PIE

Crunchy potato-topped fish pie with crème fraîche and Dijon mustard.

1 medium **potato**, peeled and cut into chunks

20g **butter**

1 fillet **salmon**, cut into chunks

1 tablespoon **olive oil**

2 tablespoons **crème fraîche**

3 **spring onions**, chopped

1/2 mug (75g) defrosted **frozen peas**

5 defrosted **frozen king prawns**

1/2 teaspoon **Dijon mustard**

1/4 mug (20g) grated **Cheddar cheese**

1. Put the potatoes in a saucepan of boiling, salted water and simmer for 8 minutes. Drain and return to the pan. Add the butter and mash.
2. Preheat the grill.
3. Meanwhile, put the salmon in a small casserole dish, season with salt and pepper, and drizzle with the olive oil.
4. Place under the grill for 5 minutes.
5. Mix together the crème fraîche, spring onions, peas, prawns and mustard.
6. Take the salmon out from under the grill and add the crème fraîche mixture.
7. Place the mashed potatoes on top and sprinkle over the cheese.
8. Place back under the grill for 5 minutes, or until the top bubbles and browns lightly.

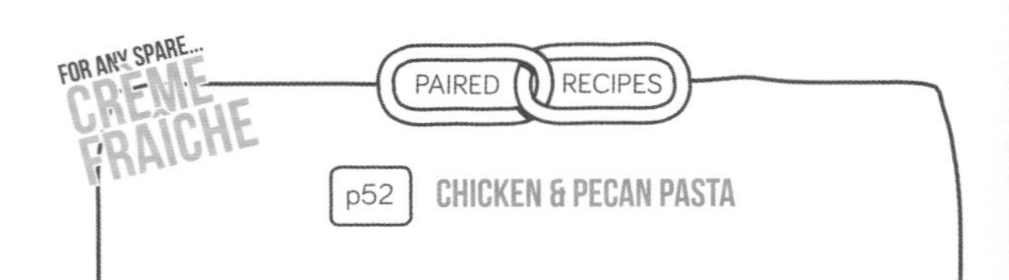

LE CREUSET

MPH KM
18
SWISS
MADE

TAKE YOUR TIME

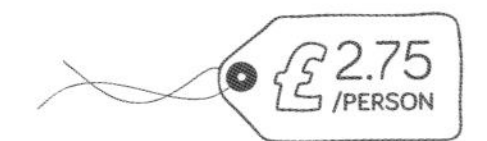

COD KEDGEREE

Korma spiced rice with spinach and flaked cod. Topped with a sliced boiled egg.

1 **egg**
1 tablespoon **olive oil**
2 **spring onions**, chopped
1/3 mug (80g) **basmati rice**
2/3 mug (200ml) **water**
1 tablespoon **Korma curry paste**
1 **cod steak**
50g **spinach**, chopped

GLUTEN-FREE OPTION: use GF curry paste.

1. Put the egg in a saucepan of boiling water and simmer for 10 minutes. Drain, rinse under cold water, and peel. Set to one side until needed.
2. Meanwhile, heat the oil in a frying pan, add the spring onions, and fry for 1 minute. Add the rice and fry for 1 minute. Add the water and curry paste and bring to the boil.
3. Simmer gently, with a lid on the pan, for 6 minutes.
4. Add the cod steak to the pan and continue to simmer, with a lid on the pan, for a further 4 minutes.
5. Take off the heat and stir in the spinach. Flake the fish and gently stir in.
6. Turn out onto a plate and place the chopped boiled egg on top.

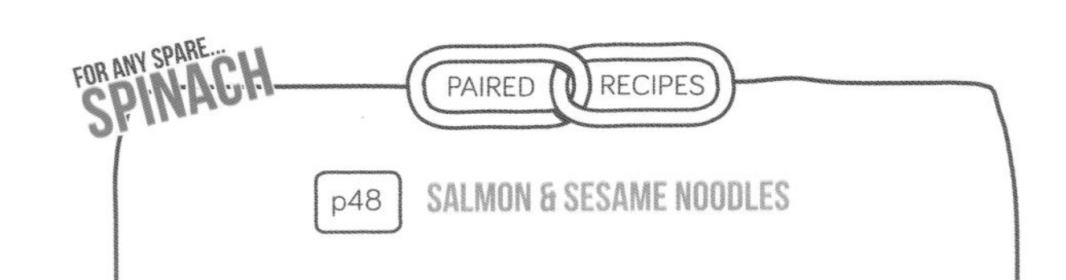

p48 SALMON & SESAME NOODLES

SAUSAGE ROAST WITH BLACKCURRANT SAUCE

Roasted vegetables and sausages with a blackcurrant jam sauce.

1 medium **potato**, cut into chunks

1 small **red onion**, peeled and halved horizontally

1 **carrot**, sliced lengthways

3 **sausages**

2 tablespoons **olive oil**

1 **tomato**, halved

SAUCE

2 teaspoons **cornflour**

1/4 mug (75ml) **water**

2 tablespoons **blackcurrant jam**

1 teaspoon **liquid veg stock**

GLUTEN-FREE OPTION: use GF stock and sausages.

VEGETARIAN OPTION: use vegetarian sausages.

1. Heat the oven to 180°C fan/200°C/gas 6.
2. Put the potatoes, onion, carrots, and sausages on a roasting tray. Drizzle with the olive oil and season well with salt and pepper.
3. Roast in the oven for 20 minutes. Add the halved tomato to the tray and roast for a further 25 minutes, or until everything is nicely browned.
4. Meanwhile, make the blackcurrant sauce. Mix the sauce ingredients together in a saucepan and bring to the boil, stirring every now and then.
5. Serve with the roast veg and sausages.

HONEY ROAST CHICKEN & FIGS

A simple, honey-roasted chicken, veg and fig dish.

Figs often come in packs of four. To use the other two, simply spread some cream cheese on toast, cut the figs in half, place on the toast, drizzle a little honey on top, and place under the grill for 2 minutes.

1 medium **potato**, cut onto chunks

2 **fresh figs**, scored across the top into four

3 **carrots**, halved lengthways

1 **chicken thigh** (with skin)

1 small **red onion**, cut into wedges

1 clove **garlic**, sliced

1 tablespoon **olive oil**

1 tablespoon **honey**

1 tablespoon **cider vinegar**

1 Preheat the oven to 200°C fan/220°C/gas 7.

2 Put the potato, figs, carrots, chicken thigh, onion and garlic on a roasting tray. Drizzle with olive oil and season with salt and pepper. Mix together and spread out evenly on the tray. Roast in the oven for 30 minutes.

3 Mix together the olive oil, honey and cider vinegar and drizzle over the top of everything. Return to the oven for a further 20 minutes, or until everything is browned.

SAUSAGE BEETROOT & BLUE CHEESE SALAD

A warm, roasted sausage and potato salad with Stilton and beetroot.

If you have any leftover beetroot, you can freeze it, see p10.

3 **sausages**

1 medium **potato**, cut into chunks

1 tablespoon **olive oil**

DRESSING

1 tablespoon **extra virgin olive oil**

2 teaspoons **cider vinegar**

2 teaspoons **honey**

salt and **pepper**

¼ bag **salad leaves** (we used rocket)

2 **spring onions**, chopped

1 **ready-cooked beetroot**, cut into sticks

25g **Stilton cheese**

1 tablespoon **roasted, chopped hazelnuts**

GLUTEN-FREE OPTION: use GF sausages.

VEGETARIAN OPTION: use vegetarian sausages.

1. Preheat the oven to 180°C fan/200°C/gas 6.
2. Put the sausages and potatoes on a roasting tray, drizzle with the oil, and season with salt and pepper. Mix together and place in the oven for 30 minutes, or until nicely browned.
3. Slice the sausages.
4. Mix the dressing ingredients together.
5. Mix together the rocket, spring onions and beetroot in a bowl. Add the potatoes and sausages to the bowl and mix.
6. Sprinkle over with the crumbled cheese and hazelnuts. Add the dressing.

THE BASIC BURGER

Simple beef burger, flavoured with red onion and Dijon mustard, served with potato wedges.

1 medium **potato**, cut into wedges

1 tablespoon **olive oil**

BURGER

125g **minced beef**

1/2 small **red onion**, finely chopped

1 **egg yolk**

1 teaspoon **Dijon mustard**

1 teaspoon **olive oil**

1 **burger bun**, lightly toasted

2 tablespoons **mayo**

1/2 **Cos lettuce**

1/2 small **red onion**, thinly sliced

1 **tomato**, sliced

GLUTEN-FREE OPTION: use GF bread or brioche bun.

1. Preheat the oven to 180°C fan/200°C/gas 6. Put the wedges on a roasting tray. Drizzle with the oil and season with salt and pepper. Mix everything together and spread out on the tray. Roast in the oven for 50 minutes.
2. In a bowl, mix together the burger ingredients, season well with salt and pepper, and form into a burger.
3. 10 minutes before the wedges are ready, heat the oil in a frying pan and fry the burger on a medium heat for 4 minutes each side. The burger should be cooked through and nicely browned.
4. Assemble the burger with the rest of the ingredients.

BEAN BURGER CRUNCH

Spiced bean burger with crushed avocado and crunchy corn chips.

Use the other half of the tin of beans, instead of borlotti beans, in the Tortilla Stacks on p182.

BURGER

1 small **red onion**, roughly chopped

1/2 x 400g tin **red kidney beans**, rinsed and drained

2 tablespoons **blanched almonds**

1/2 slice **seeded bread**

1 clove **garlic**

1 teaspoon **smoked paprika**

1/2 teaspoon **ground cumin**

1 teaspoon **liquid veg stock**

1 tablespoon **toasted sesame oil**

brioche bun, toasted

1/2 **avocado**

1/2 **Little Gem lettuce**

1 **tomato**, sliced

1 tablespoon **sweet chilli sauce**

1 small bag **corn chips**

GLUTEN-FREE OPTION: use GF stock and bread.

1. Put the burger ingredients in a processor, or use a hand-held blender and blitz. Form into a burger.
2. Heat the oil in a frying pan and fry the burger until it is nicely browned on both sides.
3. Lightly toast the brioche bun. Mash the avocado and spread on the bottom half of the brioche bun.
4. Add the burger, lettuce, tomato, chilli sauce and a few crunched up corn chips. Serve with the remaining corn chips alongside.

CHICKEN BURGER & RADISH PICKLE

Lightly spiced chicken burger with honey mayo sauce and radish pickle.

Radishes will keep quite well in the fridge for a couple of weeks; just add them, finely sliced, to salads.

RADISH PICKLE

2 tablespoons **cider vinegar**
2 teaspoons **honey**
1/4 **cucumber**, deseeded and sliced
2 **spring onions**, sliced
2 **radishes**, sliced

2 tablespoons **mayo**
1 teaspoon **honey**

BURGER

1 **chicken breast**
2 **spring onions**
1/2 teaspoon **ground ginger**
1/2 teaspoon **ground cumin**
1/2 teaspoon **ground coriander**
1/2 slice **seeded bread**

1 tablespoon **olive oil**
1 **brioche bun**

GLUTEN-FREE OPTION: use GF bread and burger bun.

1. Mix together the cider vinegar and honey and season with salt and pepper. Add the rest of the pickle ingredients. Leave to stand for 15 minutes.
2. Mix together the honey and mayo.
3. Put the burger ingredients in a food processor, or use a hand-held blender, season with salt and pepper, and blitz. Form into a burger. Just chop everything up finely if you don't have a processor.
4. Heat the oil in a frying pan and fry the burger on a medium heat until it is browned nicely on both sides and cooked through.
5. Lightly toast the brioche bun and construct the burger.

PORK BURGER & FRIED PEAR

Pork burger with fried pear and a pomegrante molasses sauce.

If you have any leftover broccoli, you can freeze it, see p10.

1 tablespoon **olive oil**

1 large **potato**, cut into chunks

125g **pork mince**

1 small **red onion**, grated

1 teaspoon **Dijon mustard**

1/2 **pear**

75g **sprouting broccoli**

SAUCE

1/4 mug (75ml) **water**

1 teaspoon **cornflour**

1 tablespoon **pomegranate molasses**

1 teaspoon **honey**

2 teaspoons **soy sauce**

GLUTEN-FREE OPTION: use GF soy sauce.

1. Heat the oil in a frying pan and gently fry the potatoes, with a lid on the pan, until they are nicely browned. You will need to keep them moving. Set aside and keep warm (perhaps under a low grill).
2. Meanwhile, mix together the mince, onion and mustard. Season well with salt and pepper and form it into a burger.
3. Add to the pan and fry the burger, on a medium heat, for 3–4 minutes each side.
4. Whilst the burger is cooking, add the pear, flat-side down, to the pan and fry until it is nicely browned. Turn over and fry on the other side.
5. Put the sprouting broccoli in a saucepan of boiling, salted water and simmer for 4 minutes. Drain and return to the pan.
6. Once the pattie and pear are done, remove from the pan, add the combined sauce ingredients, and bring to the boil.
7. Serve with the potatoes, burger, pear and broccoli.

PAPRIKA PORK BAP

Sliced pork steaks in a brioche bun with fresh, crunchy sliced apple. Served with home-made oven chips.

1 medium **potato**, cut into chips
1 tablespoon **olive oil**
1/4 teaspoon **smoked paprika**
1 **pork steak**
1 tablespoon **olive oil**
1 small **onion**, sliced
1 **bread bun/brioche bun**
1 teaspoon **Dijon mustard**
1 tablespoon **mayo**
1/2 **Little Gem lettuce**
1/2 **apple**, thinly sliced

GLUTEN-FREE OPTION: use GF bread bun.

1. Preheat the oven to 180°C fan/200°C/gas 6.
2. Put the chips on a tray, sprinkle with olive oil, and season with salt and pepper. Mix together and roast in the oven for 40 minutes, or until nicely browned.
3. 15 minutes before the end of the cooking time, rub the paprika into the pork steak and season with salt and pepper.
4. Heat the oil in a frying pan, fry the onions until they are browned and remove from the pan. Add the pork and fry for 2–3 minutes each side. Cut the pork into strips.
5. Toast the bun and spread with the mustard.
6. Spread the mayo over the top and add the lettuce and the apple.
7. Add the pork and top with the onions.
8. Serve with the chips.

MUSTARD CHICKEN & POTATO STACK

Grated potato stack with cheese-covered chicken breast and roasted cherry tomatoes. All baked in the oven (apart from the salad obviously?!).

1 medium **potato**, grated

2 **spring onions**, finely chopped

2 slices **ham**, chopped

1 teaspoon **olive oil**

1/4 mug (20g) grated **Cheddar cheese**

1 teaspoon **flour**

1 tablespoon **milk**

1/2 teaspoon **Dijon mustard**

1 **chicken breast**

6 **cherry tomatoes**

1/4 bag **salad leaves** (we used lambs lettuce)

GLUTEN-FREE OPTION: use GF flour.

1. Preheat the oven to 200°C fan/220°C/gas 7.
2. Mix together the potatoes, onions, and ham. Season well with salt and pepper. Form into a patty. Place on a greased roasting tray and brush with the oil.
3. Roast in the oven for 15 minutes.
4. Meanwhile, mix together the cheese, flour, milk and mustard. Season well with salt and pepper.
5. Once the potato stack has been in the oven for 15 minutes, add the chicken breast to the roasting tin. Pile the cheese mixture on the top and spread out to cover the chicken breast.
6. Add the tomatoes to the tray and put everything back in the oven for a further 25 minutes.
7. Serve with the lambs lettuce.

CURRIED CASHEW NUT ROAST

If you have a food processor you can put the nut roast ingredients into it and pulse a few times, but don't make it too fine. Alternatively, just chop by hand. Your choice: the chopping or the washing up of the processor.

NUT ROAST

1 small **red onion**, chopped
1/2 mug (100g) **cashew nuts**, chopped
1 slice **seeded bread**, chopped
1 tablespoon freshly chopped **basil**
1 **tomato**, chopped
1 teaspoon **liquid veg stock**
1 **egg**, beaten
2 teaspoons **Korma curry paste**

SALAD

2 **spring onions**, chopped
1/2 **Little Gem lettuce**, sliced
1/2 **apple**, sliced

DRESSING

1 teaspoon **extra virgin olive oil**
1 teaspoon **honey**
1 teaspoon **cider vinegar**

GLUTEN-FREE OPTION: use GF bread and stock.

1. Preheat the oven to 180°C fan/200°C/gas 6.
2. Grease a small casserole dish.
3. Mix together the nut roast ingredients in a bowl and transfer into the dish. Bake in the oven for 30–35 minutes. The top should be nicely browned.
4. Mix together the salad ingredients with the combined dressing ingredients, and serve with the nut roast.

CHICKEN KEBABS

Marinated chicken kebabs with pea and apricot rice.

MARINADE

1 tablespoon **olive oil**

2 tablespoons **Greek yogurt**

2 teaspoons **pomegranate molasses**

zest and juice of 1/2 **lemon**

1 **chicken breast**, cut into chunks

RICE

1/3 mug (80g) **basmati rice**

1/4 teaspoon **turmeric**

1/2 mug (75g) defrosted **frozen peas**

1 tablespoon **flaked almonds**

1 tablespoon freshly chopped **mint**

3 **ready-to-eat dried apricots**, chopped

1 tablespoon **olive oil**

VEGETARIAN OPTION: use 100g Quorn chicken-style pieces.

1. Mix together the marinade ingredients. Add the chicken and mix together. Leave to marinate for 15 minutes. Season with salt and pepper.
2. Meanwhile, put the rice and turmeric in a saucepan with 2/3 mug of boiling water. Simmer gently, with a lid on the pan, for 10 minutes.
3. Add the rest of the rice ingredients and mix. Leave to stand with the lid on the pan.
4. Put the chicken on a skewer. Heat the oil in a frying pan. Add the chicken to the pan and fry on a medium heat for 5–6 minutes. Turn the skewer as the chicken browns. Remove the skewer from the pan, add the rest of the marinade, and simmer for 1 minute.
5. Serve the chicken skewer on top of the rice and pour over the sauce.

NEXT LEVEL JACKET POTATO

To use the other half of the tin of beans, make 'Beans on Toast'. Heat ½ tablespoon of olive oil in a saucepan, add half a chopped onion and fry for 1 minute. Add the beans, 1 tablespoon of tomato purée and 1 tablespoon of water and simmer together for 2 minutes. Season with salt and pepper and serve on the toast.

1 medium **potato**, with a cross cut into the top

1 small **red onion**, peeled and halved

2 tablespoons **toasted sesame oil**

125g **mushrooms**, sliced

1 clove **garlic**, sliced

BAKED BEANS

½ x 400g tin **haricot beans**, rinsed and drained

1 tablespoon **sundried tomato purée**

2 teaspoons **honey**

1 tablespoon **cider vinegar**

1 tablespoon **water**

10g **butter**

1. Preheat the oven to 200°C fan/220°C/gas 7.
2. Put the potato and onion on a roasting tray and drizzle with the oil. Season with salt and pepper and roast in the oven for 35 minutes.
3. Add the mushrooms and garlic to the roasting tray and drizzle with oil. Roast for a further 25 minutes until everything is browned.
4. 5 minutes before the end of the cooking time, put the baked bean ingredients in a saucepan and heat through.
5. Take out of the oven and transfer to a plate. Add the butter to the potato and add the beans.

HARISSA ROASTED CHICKEN

Harissa chicken with roasted vegetables served with coriander yogurt. A 'hands-off' meal where you just whack everything in the oven at various times and let the flavours come to life.

2 **parsnips**, peeled and cut into chunks

1 small **red onion**, cut into wedges

2 **carrots**, cut into chunks

1 clove **garlic**, sliced

1 **tomato**, halved

2 teaspoons **harissa paste**

1 tablespoon **olive oil**

1 **chicken breast**

1 teaspoon **harissa paste**

2 teaspoons **olive oil**

1 tablespoon freshly chopped **coriander**

2 tablespoons **Greek yogurt**

1. Preheat the oven to 180°C fan/200°C/gas 6.
2. Put the parsnips, onion, carrots, garlic and tomato on a roasting tray. Add the harissa paste and the olive oil, season well with salt and pepper and mix everything together. Spread out and roast in the oven for 20 minutes.
3. After 20 minutes, take the chicken breast and rub the harissa paste and the olive oil into it. Season with salt and pepper and add to the roasting tray. Roast for a further 20 minutes.
4. Serve with the combined coriander and yogurt.

SWEET OR SAVOURY BACON & EGG BAKE

Is this breakfast or lunch, sweet or savoury? You decide! Serve it with either maple syrup, Tabasco sauce or some sweet chilli sauce.

1 slice **seeded bread**
2 **eggs**
¼ mug (75ml) **milk**
½ teaspoon **Dijon mustard**
½ mug (40g) grated **Cheddar cheese**
4 rashers **bacon**

SELECT A TOPPING:

Tabasco sauce
or
sweet chilli sauce
or
maple syrup

GLUTEN-FREE OPTION: use GF bread.

1. Preheat the oven to 180°C fan/200°C/gas 6.
2. Cut the slice of bread into four pieces.
3. Beat the eggs and add the milk, mustard and grated cheese.
4. Put the bread in a casserole dish and pour the egg mixture over.
5. Scrunch up the bacon and arrange on the top.
6. Bake in the oven for 35 minutes.
7. Serve with either Tabasco sauce, sweet chilli sauce or maple syrup.

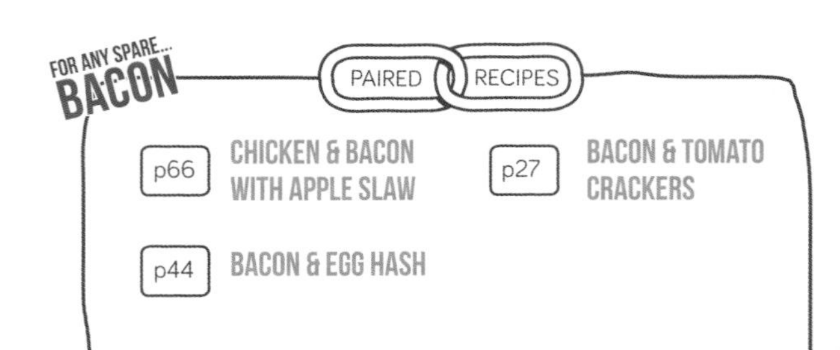

CHICKEN SCHNITZEL

Cinnamon and nutmeg crusted chicken schnitzel with a simple salad and honey mayo dressing.

1 **chicken breast**

1 slice **bread**, made into breadcrumbs

pinch of **cinnamon**

pinch of **nutmeg**

1 **egg**, beaten

1 tablespoon **olive oil**

SALAD

1/2 **Little Gem lettuce**, sliced

1/4 **cucumber**, thinly sliced

2 **spring onions**, thinly sliced

DRESSING

1 tablespoon **mayo**

1/2 teaspoon **honey**

1 teaspoon **cider vinegar**

salt and **pepper**

GLUTEN-FREE OPTION: use GF bread.

1. Put the chicken breast between 2 pieces of baking paper and bash with a rolling pin, or something similarly heavy, until it is approximately 1cm thick.
2. Mix together the breadcrumbs with the cinnamon and nutmeg and season with salt and pepper. Put on a plate.
3. Put the beaten egg in a small bowl and dip the chicken into it. Press the chicken into the plate of breadcrumbs and coat evenly on both sides.
4. Heat the olive oil in a frying pan and add the chicken. Fry on a low heat for 2 minutes each side. Check that the chicken is cooked through. The breadcrumbs should be golden brown.
5. Mix the salad ingredients together and add the combined dressing.

'NO-PASTRY' SALMON & AVOCADO TART

Simple 'tart' with a salmon, avocado and chive filling. No need to make pastry.

2 slices **bread**, crusts cut off

10g **butter**, melted

juice of 1/4 **lemon**

1 tablespoon **mayo**

1 teaspoon freshly chopped **chives**

100g tin **salmon**, drained

1/2 **avocado**, cut into chunks

1/4 bag **salad leaves** (we used rocket)

DRESSING

2 teaspoons **extra virgin olive oil**

1 teaspoon **honey**

2 teaspoons **cider vinegar**

GLUTEN-FREE OPTION: use GF bread.

1. Preheat the oven to 180°C fan/200°C/gas 6. Brush the bread with the melted butter. Press into a ramekin and bake in the oven for 15 minutes, or until the bread is crispy.
2. In a bowl, mix together the lemon, mayo and chives and season with salt and pepper. Gently flake the salmon and stir in with the avocado.
3. Take the bread out of the ramekin and put in the salmon mix.
4. Serve with the salad leaves and the combined dressing ingredients.

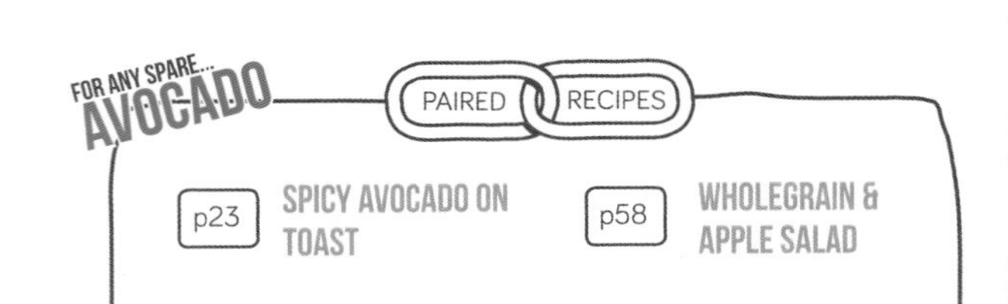

p23 SPICY AVOCADO ON TOAST
p58 WHOLEGRAIN & APPLE SALAD

COD & CHIPS

Flaked almond and breadcrumb coated cod loin with chips. Served with roasted cherry tomatoes and sundried tomato mayo.

1 medium **potato**, cut into chips

1 tablespoon **olive oil**

1 slice **bread**, made into breadcrumbs

1 tablespoon **flaked almonds**

1 **cod loin**

6 **cherry tomatoes**

1 tablespoon **olive oil**

2 tablespoons **mayo**

1 teaspoon **sundried tomato purée**

GLUTEN-FREE OPTION: use GF bread.

1. Preheat the oven to 180°C fan/200°C/gas 6.
2. Put the chips on a roasting tray, drizzle with 1 tablespoon of olive oil and season with salt and pepper. Mix everything together and spread out, leaving space for the fish to be added later.
3. Roast in the oven for 25 minutes.
4. Mix together the breadcrumbs and almonds and season with salt and pepper. Press onto the fish.
5. Once the potatoes have been in the oven for 25 minutes, add the fish and tomatoes to the roasting tray. Drizzle the other tablespoon of olive oil over the tomatoes and season with salt and pepper. Return to the oven for a further 20 minutes.
6. Meanwhile, mix together the mayo and tomato purée.
7. Serve everything together.

LASAGNE

It's a lasagne, a lovely simple one, just for you.

2 **dried lasagne sheets**
15g **butter**
1 tablespoon **flour**
½ mug (150ml) **milk**
75g **cream cheese with garlic and herbs**
1 tablespoon **olive oil**
1 small **red onion**, chopped
125g **minced beef**
2 **tomatoes**, chopped
1 tablespoon freshly chopped **basil**
2 teaspoons **tomato purée**
2 tablespoons **water**
1 teaspoon **liquid veg stock**
¼ mug (15g) grated **Parmesan cheese** for the top

GLUTEN-FREE OPTION: use GF lasagne sheets, flour and stock.

VEGETARIAN OPTION: use Quorn mince and Parmesan-style cheese.

1. Preheat the oven to 180°C fan/200°C/gas 6.
2. Break each lasagne sheet in half to make 4 pieces.
3. To make the cheese sauce, heat the butter in a saucepan and add the flour, mix well and heat for 1 minute. Add the milk and cream cheese and bring to the boil. Season with salt and pepper and set to one side until needed.
4. Heat the olive oil in the frying pan, add the onions and fry until they begin to soften.
5. Add the mince and fry until no longer pink.
6. Add the tomatoes and cook until they begin to fall apart. Add the rest of the ingredients, apart from the Parmesan. Bring to the boil and then simmer for 2 minutes.
7. Arrange the tomato sauce, lasagne sheets and cheese sauce in layers, finishing with the cheese sauce.
8. Sprinkle the Parmesan over the top and cook in the oven for 35 minutes.

FOUR IN ONE

The idea of 'Four-in-One' is that on Day One you cook a 'Master Ingredient' which is then used in four different dishes.

Some things seem impossible to do just for one - a lovely beef brisket, a roast chicken, or roasting whole butternut squashes - without lots left over.

The beauty of 'four-in-one' meals is that, with the master ingredient, you can create incredibly tasty dishes in minutes. It opens up meal opportunities which would normally seem totally unrealistic, for example, a quick salad using slow roasted beef.

ONE-POT SUNDAY ROAST

Everyone loves a roast. Four days in a row though?? Thought not. Here is a way of having a roast one day and then using the leftovers in three completely different meals over the next few days.

1.5kg **whole chicken**

2 medium **potatoes**, cut into chunks

1 small **red onion**, cut into wedges

2 **carrots**, peeled and cut into wedges

3 sprigs **rosemary**

2 tablespoons **olive oil**

10g **butter**

2 teaspoons **flour**

GLUTEN-FREE OPTION: use GF flour.

1. Preheat the oven to 180°C fan/200°C/gas 6.
2. Put the chicken on a roasting tray along with the potatoes, onion, carrots and rosemary.
3. Drizzle with olive oil, add 1/3 mug water, and season well with salt and pepper. Cover with foil and roast in the oven for 1 hour.
4. After 1 hour, remove the foil and roast for a further 45 minutes, or until everything is browned.
5. To make the gravy, melt the butter in a saucepan, add the flour and mix well. Add the juices from the roasting tray, plus 1/3 of a mug of water, and bring to the boil. The gravy should thicken.

ROAST CHICKEN #1 OF 4

Recipe #2 on next page → → →

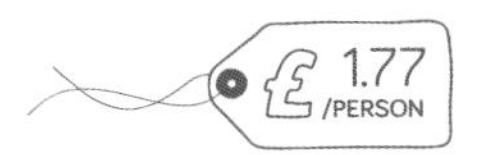

ROAST CHICKEN SALAD

A quick and easy, roast chicken salad with pecan nuts and Dijon mustard dressing.

1 portion leftover **roast chicken**, see p168

1/2 **avocado**

1/2 **Little Gem lettuce**

1 **spring onion**, chopped

6 **cherry tomatoes**, halved

5 **pecan nuts**, roughly chopped

DRESSING

2 tablespoons **mayo**

1 tablespoon **extra virgin olive oil**

juice of 1/4 **lemon**

1/2 teaspoon **Dijon mustard**

1 teaspoon **honey**

salt and **pepper**

1. Tear the chicken into bite-sized pieces.
2. Cut the avocado in half and peel one half. Cut into small chunks. Save the half with the stone in and cover with cling film.
3. Mix together the chicken, avocado, lettuce, spring onions and cherry tomatoes and place in a bowl.
4. Mix together the dressing ingredients and drizzle over the salad. Sprinkle the pecans over.

ROAST CHICKEN #2 OF 4

#3 of 4 recipe on next page

VINEYARD CHICKEN RISOTTO

You didn't read that wrong. These are not black olives, they are grapes…in a risotto. Try it!!

1 tablespoon **olive oil**

2 **spring onions**, chopped

1 clove **garlic**, chopped

75g **mushrooms**, sliced

1/3 mug (70g) **risotto rice**

2/3 mug (200ml) **water**

1/4 teaspoon **dried rosemary** (or fresh if you have any left)

2 teaspoons **liquid chicken stock**

1 portion leftover **roast chicken**, see p168, roughly chopped

1/4 mug (15g) grated **Parmesan cheese**

75g **red grapes**, halved

1 teaspoon freshly chopped **basil**

GLUTEN-FREE OPTION: use GF stock.

1. Heat the oil in a frying pan and add the onions and garlic. Fry for 1 minute.
2. Add the mushrooms and fry for 2 minutes.
3. Add the rice and fry for 1 minute. Add the water, rosemary and stock. Simmer gently, with a lid on the pan, for 10 minutes, stirring occasionally.
4. Add the chicken and heat for 1 minute.
5. Add the Parmesan and stir. Add the grapes and stir once.
6. Serve with the basil on top.

ROAST CHICKEN #3 OF 4

#4 of 4 recipe on next page

SWEET & SOUR CHICKEN NOODLES

Using the ready-roasted peppers in a jar, makes it very quick and easy and avoids having half a regular pepper hanging around the fridge.

50g **dried rice noodles**

1 tablespoon **toasted sesame oil**

2 **spring onions**, chopped

1 clove **garlic**, chopped

1/2 **red apple**, chopped

75g **mushrooms**, sliced

1/2 **ready-roasted red pepper** (from a jar), chopped

SAUCE

2 teaspoons **soy sauce**

2 teaspoons **cider vinegar**

2 teaspoons **maple syrup**

2 teaspoons **tomato purée**

1 teaspoon **liquid chicken stock**

1/3 mug (100ml) **water** + 1 teaspoon **cornflour**

1 portion leftover **roast chicken**, see p168, chopped

GLUTEN-FREE OPTION: use GF soy sauce and stock.

1. Put the noodles in a bowl and cover with boiling water. Leave to stand for 10 minutes and then drain.
2. Meanwhile, heat the oil in a frying pan. Add the onions, garlic, and apple and fry for 1 minute.
3. Add the mushrooms and peppers and fry for 2 minutes.
4. Mix together the sauce ingredients, add to the pan, along with the chicken, and simmer for 2 minutes.
5. Serve with the drained noodles.

ROAST CHICKEN #4 OF 4

SPAGHETTI BOLOGNESE

This dish is good enough to make us break our rule for this book of only using two small pans. You'll need a large frying pan, or wok, for this one. Enjoy!

50g **spaghetti**
1 tablespoon **olive oil**
1 **onion**, chopped
2 cloves **garlic**, chopped
500g **minced beef**
6 **tomatoes**, chopped
250g **mushrooms**, sliced
2 tablespoons **tomato purée**
1 tablespoon **liquid beef stock**
½ mug (150ml) **water**

GLUTEN-FREE OPTION: use GF stock and spaghetti.

VEGETARIAN OPTION: use Quorn mince and veg stock.

1. Put the spaghetti in a saucepan of boiling, salted water, simmer for 10 minutes, and then drain.
2. Meanwhile, heat the oil in a large frying pan or wok. Add the onions and garlic and fry until the onions begin to soften.
3. Add the minced beef and fry until the mince is no longer pink.
4. Add the tomatoes and mushrooms and fry for 3–4 minutes.
5. Add the rest of the ingredients and season well with salt and pepper. Simmer for 5 minutes.
6. Serve ¼ of the sauce with the spaghetti.

BOLOGNESE #1 OF 4

#2 of 4 recipe on next page

SPICED PASTA BAKE

Paprika and cumin spiced beef and pasta bake, using the Bolognese sauce.

²/₃ mug (70g) **pasta** (we used fusilli)

1 portion **Bolognese sauce**, see p176

½ **ready-roasted red pepper** (from a jar), chopped

1 teaspoon **smoked paprika**

1 teaspoon **ground cumin**

½ mug (40g) grated **Cheddar cheese**

GLUTEN-FREE OPTION: use GF stock and pasta.

VEGETARIAN OPTION: use Quorn mince and veg stock.

1. Preheat the grill.
2. Put the pasta in a saucepan of boiling, salted water. Simmer for 10 minutes, drain and return to the pan.
3. Put the Bolognese sauce in a saucepan, together with the pepper, paprika and cumin. Simmer for 5 minutes.
4. Add the pasta and mix together.
5. Pour into a small casserole dish and sprinkle the cheese on top.
6. Place under the grill until the cheese melts and bubbles.

BOLOGNESE #2 OF 4

#3 of 4 recipe on next page

INSIDE-OUT BAKED POTATO

The tallest Shepherds Pie ever. It takes a degree in architecture to get this all piled up, but it's fun to do, and will taste just the same if it collapses on you!

1 large **potato**

1 portion **Bolognese sauce**, see p176

1 teaspoon **wholegrain mustard**

10g **butter**

1/4 mug (20g) grated **Cheddar cheese**

GLUTEN-FREE OPTION: use GF stock.

VEGETARIAN OPTION: use Quorn mince and veg stock.

1 Preheat the oven to 180°C fan/200°C/gas 6. Put the potato on a baking tray, slice a cross in the top, and bake in the oven for 50 minutes.

2 Once the potato is cooked, take out of the oven and slice off the very top. Scoop out the potato and mix together with the butter. Season with salt and pepper.

3 Preheat the grill.

4 Put the portion of Bolognese sauce in a saucepan and bring to the boil. Add the mustard. Make sure the sauce is heated through.

5 Put the beef mixture in the potato skin and gently pile the potato on top. Sprinkle the grated cheese over and place under the grill until the cheese bubbles and browns a little.

BOLOGNESE #3 OF 4

#4 of 4 recipe on next page

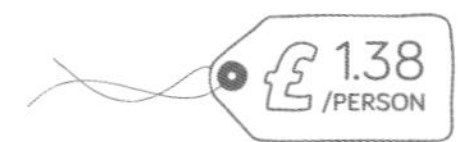

TORTILLA STACK

Use the rest of the beans for 'Beans on Toast'. Just heat 1 tablespoon of olive oil in a frying pan, add 1/4 teaspoon each of cumin, coriander and paprika. Add the beans and fry for 1 minute. Push them to one side, but leave in the pan. Add and egg and fry until the white is cooked, but the yolk runny. Serve on toast.

1 portion **Bolognese sauce**, see p176

1 tablespoon **tomato purée**

2 tablespoons **water**

1/2 x 400g tin **borlotti beans**, rinsed and drained

1/2 **fat red chilli**, chopped

1 **tortilla**

1/2 mug (40g) grated **Cheddar cheese**

GLUTEN-FREE OPTION: use GF tortillas.

VEGETARIAN OPTION: use Quorn mince and veg stock.

1. Preheat the grill.
2. Put the Bolognese sauce in a saucepan, with the water, tomato purée, beans and chilli, and simmer for 5 minutes.
3. Cut the tortilla into 4.
4. Place one piece on a greased, baking tray, add 1/4 of the sauce, another piece of tortilla and another 1/4 of the sauce and so on. Sprinkle the grated cheese over the top and place under the grill until the cheese bubbles and browns a little.

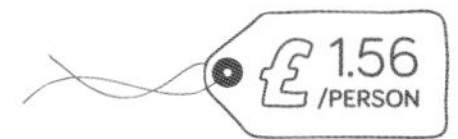

ROAST SQUASH SALAD

We've made this one the 'Master Recipe' but in reality you can start with any of the four recipes, once you've roasted the squash.

1 **butternut squash**, peeled and cut into chunks

1 tablespoon **olive oil**

SALAD

1/2 bag **salad leaves** (we used lambs lettuce)

2 **spring onions**, chopped

6 **cherry tomatoes**, halved

50g **feta cheese**, cubed

DRESSING

2 teaspoons **pomegranate molasses**

2 teaspoons **extra virgin olive oil**

juice of 1/4 **lemon**

1. Preheat the oven to 180°C fan/200°C/gas 6.
2. Drizzle the squash pieces with the olive oil, mix together, and season well with salt and pepper.
3. Roast in the oven for 45 minutes, or until lightly browned and tender. Set 3/4 of the squash to one side to cool and store in the fridge until you need it.
4. Mix the roasted squash with the rest of the salad ingredients.
5. Mix the dressing ingredients together and drizzle over.

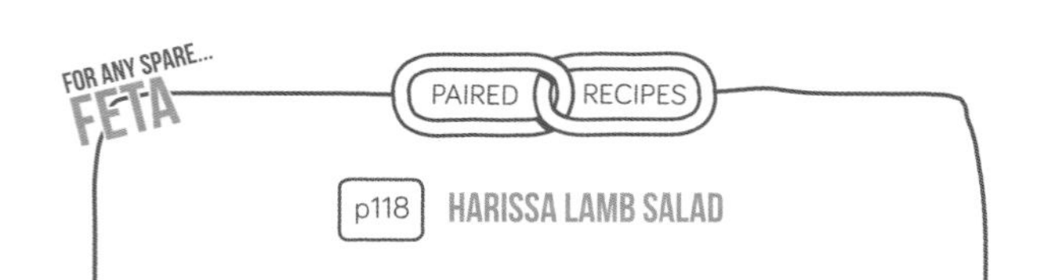

SQUASH #1 OF 4
#2 of 4 recipe on next page

RED THAI BUTTERNUT SOUP

Super-speedy, Thai butternut squash soup with seeded bread croutons.

1 tablespoon **olive oil**

1 small **red onion**, chopped

1 teaspoon **Thai red curry paste**

1/2 teaspoon **liquid veg stock**

3/4 mug (225ml) **water**

1 portion **roasted butternut squash**, see p184

1/4 mug (75ml) **single cream**

1 slice **seeded bread**

1 tablespoon freshly chopped **coriander**

GLUTEN-FREE OPTION: use GF stock and bread.

1. Heat the oil in a saucepan. Add the onion and fry until they begin to brown.
2. Add the curry paste, stock and water. Simmer for 2 minutes.
3. Add the butternut squash and simmer for 2 minutes.
4. Blitz with a hand-held blender and stir in the cream.
5. Toast the bread and serve with the coriander sprinkled over.

SQUASH #2 OF 4

#3 of 4 recipe on next page

SQUASH & PEPPER PASTA

See p10 for what you can do if you have excess cream after cooking this one. Don't worry, it doesn't have to go to waste.

2/3 mug (65g) **pasta** (we used fusilli)

2 teaspoons **olive oil**

1 small **red onion**, sliced

1 clove **garlic**, chopped

1 portion **roasted butternut squash**, see p184

1 **ready-roasted red pepper** (from a jar), chopped

2 tablespoons **single cream**

1/4 mug (20g) grated **Cheddar cheese**

GLUTEN-FREE OPTION: use GF pasta.

1. Put the pasta in a saucepan of boiling, salted water. Simmer for 8 minutes. Drain and return to the pan.
2. Preheat the grill.
3. Meanwhile, heat the oil in a frying pan and add the onion and garlic. Fry for 2–3 minutes until the onion begins to soften.
4. Add the cooked pasta, squash, peppers and cream. Heat through.
5. Top with the grated cheese. Put under the grill until the cheese bubbles and begins to brown.

SQUASH #3 OF 4

#4 of 4 recipe on next page

GF OPTION V

SQUASH CURRY & RAITA

Roasted butternut squash curry with Greek yogurt, cucumber and mint raita.

1/3 mug (80g) **basmati rice**
1 tablespoon **olive oil**
1 small **red onion**, sliced
1 clove **garlic**, chopped
2 teaspoons freshly grated **ginger**
1/2 **fat red chilli**, chopped
1 teaspoon **ground cumin**
1 teaspoon **ground coriander**
1/4 mug (75ml) **water**
1/2 teaspoon **liquid veg stock**
1 portion **roasted butternut squash**, see p184

RAITA

2 tablespoons **Greek yogurt**
1/4 **cucumber**, grated
1 tablespoon freshly chopped **mint**

GLUTEN-FREE OPTION: use GF stock.

1. Put the rice in a saucepan with 2/3 mug of boiling water. Simmer gently, with a lid on the pan, for 10 minutes.
2. Meanwhile, heat the oil in a frying pan, add the onions, garlic, ginger and chilli and fry for 2 minutes.
3. Add the cumin and coriander and fry for 1 minute.
4. Add the water and stock and simmer for 3 minutes.
5. Add the squash and simmer for 2 minutes to thicken slightly.
6. Mix together the raita ingredients and serve with the curry and rice.

ROAST BEEF DINNER

Love roast beef, but don't want to have to deal with all the leftovers? You don't need to eat Sunday Roast four days in a row. Make use of that lovely meat in the following four recipes. Use just 1/4 of the meat in this meal and the rest in the recipes that follow.

1 kg **beef brisket**

1 **sprig rosemary**

1/2 mug (150ml) **water**

2 tablespoons **olive oil**

1 large **potato**, cut into chunks

1 small **red onion**, cut into wedges

2 **carrots**, cut into chunks

75g **sprouting broccoli**

10g softened **butter**

2 teaspoons **flour**

GLUTEN-FREE OPTION: use GF flour.

1 Preheat the oven to 180°C fan/200°C/gas 6.

2 Put the brisket in a roasting tray along with the rosemary and water. Drizzle with olive oil and season well with salt and pepper. Cover with foil and roast in the oven for 1 hour. After 1 hour, turn down the oven to 160°C fan/180°C/gas 4 and cook for a further 2 hours.

3 1 hour before the end of the cooking-time, put the potatoes, onions and carrots on a roasting tray. Drizzle with olive oil and season well with salt and pepper. Roast in the oven alongside the meat. Take the meat out and leave to rest in the juices. Turn the oven back up to 180°C fan/200°C/gas 6 and roast for another 30 minutes.

4 5 minutes before the end of the cooking-time, put the broccoli in a saucepan of boiling, salted water and simmer for 5 minutes.

5 To make the gravy, put the butter and flour into a saucepan, mix well and heat thoroughly. Add the juices from the roasting tray and bring to the boil. Use half the gravy for the roast dinner and the other half for the Beef Pesto Pasta, see p198.

BEEF BRISKET #1 OF 4

#2 of 4 recipe on next page

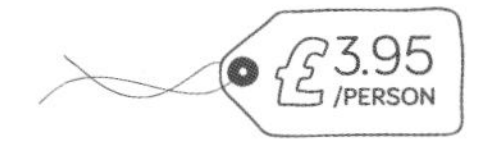

ROAST BEEF SALAD

How else could you get a 'quick', blue cheese salad with 'slow' roast beef? Use our 'four-in-one' approach. Use any excess blue cheese you may have on toast with some good chutney.

1 portion **roast beef**, see p192, roughly chopped
1 **Little Gem lettuce**
2 **spring onions**, chopped
1/4 **cucumber**, chopped

DRESSING

1 tablespoon **extra virgin olive oil**
1 tablespoon **cider vinegar**
2 teaspoons **honey**

75g **blue cheese**

1. Mix together the beef, lettuce, spring onions and cucumber.
2. Mix the dressing ingredients and add to the beef mixture.
3. Put on a plate and crumble the cheese over the top.

BEEF BRISKET #2 OF 4

#3 of 4 recipe on next page

QUICK BEEF CURRY

Roasted beef curry made in 15 minutes!! Enjoy high levels of smugness as you tuck into this one, having roasted your beef a couple of days ago.

1/3 mug (80g) **basmati rice**

1 tablespoon **olive oil**

1 small **red onion**, chopped

1 clove **garlic**, chopped

75g **mushrooms**, sliced

1 portion **roast beef**, see p192, roughly chopped,

1 tablespoon **Rogan Josh curry paste**

165ml tin **coconut milk**

1/2 **ready-roasted red pepper** (from a jar), chopped

GLUTEN-FREE OPTION: use GF curry paste.

1. Put the rice in a saucepan with 2/3 mug of boiling water. Simmer gently, with a lid on the pan, for 10 minutes.
2. Meanwhile, heat the oil in a frying pan and add the onions and garlic. Fry for 1 minute.
3. Add the mushrooms and beef and fry for 2 minutes.
4. Add the curry paste and coconut milk and simmer for 2 minutes.
5. Add the peppers and simmer for 1 minute.
6. Serve with the rice.

BEEF BRISKET #3 OF 4

#4 of 4 recipe on next page

BEEF PESTO PASTA

It would be worth the effort of making the roast beef just to get to this little pesto pasta dish; the three other recipes are a nice little bonus though!

2/3 mug (70g) **pasta** (we used fusilli)

1 tablespoon **olive oil**

2 **spring onions**, sliced

1 clove **garlic**, chopped

2 tablespoons **green pesto**

1 portion **roast beef**, see p192, roughly chopped

75g **mushrooms**, sliced

half of the gravy from the **roast beef meal**, see p192

GLUTEN-FREE OPTION: use GF pasta.

1. Put the pasta in a saucepan of boiling, salted water. Bring to the boil and then simmer for 8 minutes. Drain, but retain 2 tablespoons of the cooking liquid.

2. Heat the oil in a frying pan and add the onions and garlic. Fry for 2 minutes.

3. Add the pesto, beef, mushrooms and gravy. Heat for 2 minutes.

4. Mix in the pasta and heat for 1 minute. Add the saved pasta liquid if the pasta and beef mix looks dry.

SWEEEE

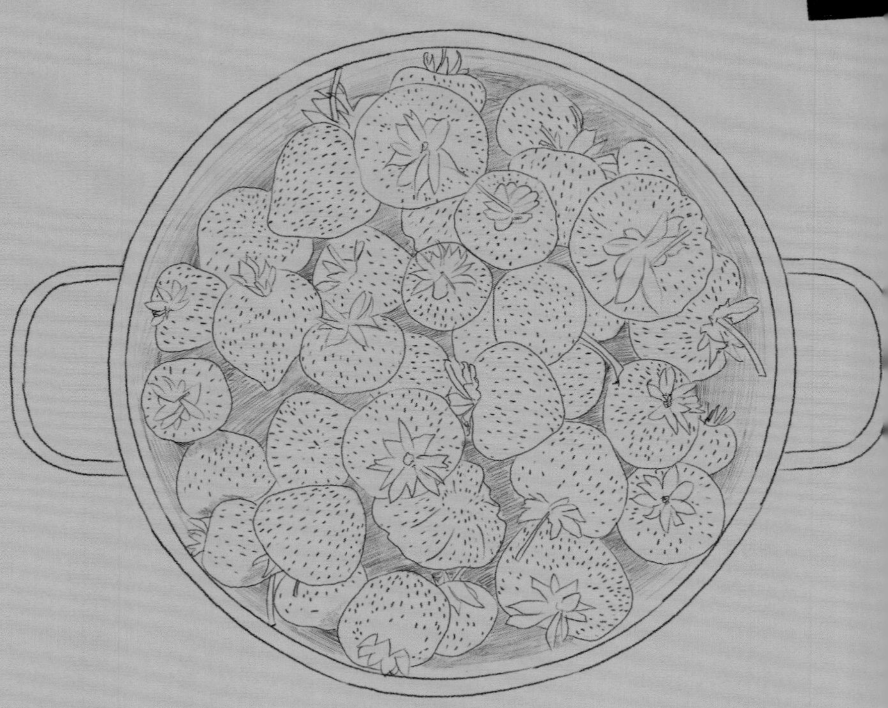

EEEEEET

BROWNIE IN A MUG

Who doesn't like brownies? But you don't always want to make a whole tray full of them. These are ready in about a minute. Mixed and cooked in a mug, so hardly any washing up either. What a winner!

15g **butter**

2 tablespoons **soft brown sugar**

2 1/2 tablespoons **self-raising flour**

2 tablespoons **cocoa powder**

1 tablespoon **milk**

60g **dark chocolate**, chopped roughly

GLUTEN-FREE OPTION: use GF flour.

1. Put the butter and sugar into a mug. Microwave for 10 seconds at a time, stirring in between. Repeat until the sugar is no longer 'gritty'.
2. Add the flour, cocoa and milk (add another tablespoon of milk if you want it nice and soggy in the middle) and stir well.
3. Stir in half the chocolate.
4. Put the rest of the chocolate on the top.
5. Put in the microwave for 40 seconds.
6. Serve with ice cream or cream, whichever you have to hand.

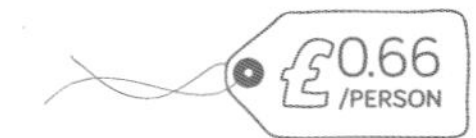

PEANUT BUTTER & BANANA YOGURT

Tim has this all the time when he wants something really quick, and it's pretty much guilt-free if you choose 'good' honey (as you know, we recommend raw honey). Easy to whip up and with an added crunch from the peanut butter and cashews.

6 tablespoons **Greek yogurt**

1 tablespoon good quality **crunchy peanut butter**

1 **banana**, sliced

2 tablespoons **cashew nuts**, crushed

1 teaspoon **honey**

1. Mix the yogurt and peanut butter together. Put in a bowl.
2. Add the banana and sprinkle over the nuts. Drizzle over the honey.

DECONSTRUCTED CHEESECAKE

All the elements of a cheesecake without the hassle of moulds.

You can freeze excess double cream, see p10.

25g **butter**

3 **digestive biscuits**

3 tablespoons (45ml) **double cream**

2 tablespoons **cream cheese**

1 teaspoon **icing sugar**

zest and juice of 1/4 **lemon**

75g **raspberries**

GLUTEN FREE OPTION: use GF biscuits.

1. Melt the butter in a saucepan.
2. Put the digestive biscuits in a plastic bag and crush them with the rolling pin. Add to the melted butter and mix. Turn out onto a small plate, push the crumbs together as much as you like. Leave in the fridge while you make the topping.
3. Beat the cream with a whisk until stiff. Fold in the cream cheese and icing sugar. Add the lemon zest and juice and mix. Spoon the mixture on top of the biscuit base.
4. Take half the raspberries and place on top of the cheesecake. Take the other half and place in a fine sieve. Press through with the back of a spoon to make a 'jus'. Pour that over the top.
5. Leave in the fridge for 1 hour, until it is cool and set properly, or if you are impatient, just eat it straight away!

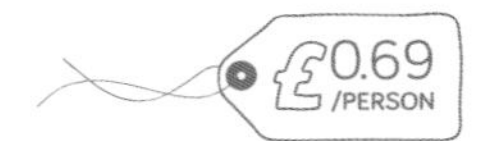

GF V

CINNAMON FRIED BANANA & YOGURT

Banana, fried in honey and cinnamon, served with Greek yogurt and hazelnuts. A great treat for when you have a banana that needs 'using up'.

20g **butter**

1 teaspoon **honey**

pinch of **cinnamon**

1 **banana**, sliced

4 tablespoons **Greek yogurt**

1 tablespoon **roasted chopped hazelnuts**

1. Gently heat the butter and honey in a frying pan and add the cinnamon.
2. Add the banana to the pan and fry gently for 2 minutes.
3. Serve with the Greek yogurt and top with the nuts.

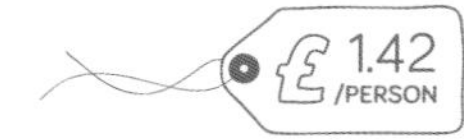

COCONUT RICE & PEAR PUDDING

Coconut milk, lime and maple syrup rice pudding with sliced pear and hazelnuts.

1/4 mug (70g) **risotto rice**
165ml tin **coconut milk**
1/4 mug (75ml) **water**
1 tablespoon **maple syrup**
zest and juice of 1/2 **lime**
1/2 **pear**, cored and sliced (we used Williams)
2 teaspoons **roasted chopped hazelnuts**
2 teaspoons **maple syrup**

1. Put the rice, coconut milk and water in a saucepan and bring to the boil. Simmer very gently, with a lid on the pan, for 12 minutes, or until the rice is tender. Stir frequently.
2. Add the maple syrup and the lime zest and juice. Stir together.
3. Serve with the pear and nuts and drizzle over with maple syrup.

ETON MESS

A classic British, summer dessert, ridiculously simple to make, but a winner every time.

We are sure you will find a 'use' for the other half of the Mars bar. Any excess meringue nests you have will keep in your store cupboard for ages, ready to use at a moment's notice.

You can freeze any excess cream, see p10.

1/3 mug (100ml) **double cream**

1/4 teaspoon **vanilla bean paste**

1 **meringue nest**

6 **strawberries**, chopped

1/2 x 58g **Mars Bar**, chopped

1. Put the cream into a large bowl and beat until it thickens.
2. Stir in the vanilla bean paste.
3. Crumble the meringue and add to the bowl, along with the chopped strawberries and Mars Bar. Stir together.
4. Serve in a bowl.
5. There may be enough for more than one serving. However, the Eton Mess does need to be eaten straight away, or the meringue dissolves.

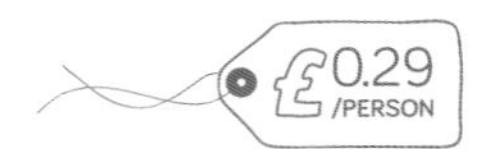

APPLE CRUMBLE

Apple and cinnamon crumble served with cream or ice cream. Enjoy!

You can freeze any excess cream, see p10.

1/2 **apple**, cored and chopped into chunks

1/4 mug (75ml) **water**

1 tablespoon **soft brown sugar**

2 tablespoons **flour**

10g **butter**

1 tablespoon **oats**

pinch of **cinnamon**

1 tablespoon **soft brown sugar**

double cream, or **ice cream**, to serve

GLUTEN-FREE OPTION: use GF flour and oats.

1. Preheat the oven to 180°C fan/200°C/gas 6.
2. Put the apple in a saucepan with the water. Simmer for 5 minutes. Add the sugar and mix. Place in the bottom of a greased, ramekin dish.
3. Put the flour and butter in a small bowl and gently rub in the butter, until you have something resembling breadcrumbs.
4. Add the oats, cinnamon and sugar and mix.
5. Put the oat mixture on top of the apples.
6. Bake in the oven for 25 minutes.
7. Serve with cream or ice cream.

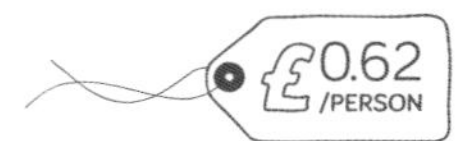

BREAD & BUTTER PUDDING

Brioche bread and butter pudding with fruits of the forest.

1 **brioche bun**, sliced

1/4 mug (35g) defrosted **frozen fruits of the forest**

1 **egg**, beaten

1/4 mug (75ml) **milk**

2 teaspoons **honey**

GLUTEN-FREE OPTION: use GF brioche.

1. Preheat the oven to 180°C fan/200°C/gas 6. Grease a ramekin dish.
2. Put the brioche into the dish, see photo. Add the fruit and tuck between the bread pieces.
3. Mix together the beaten egg, milk and honey. Pour over the dish. Leave to stand for 10 minutes to allow the bread to absorb the egg mixture.
4. Bake in the oven for 25 minutes. The top should be nicely browned.

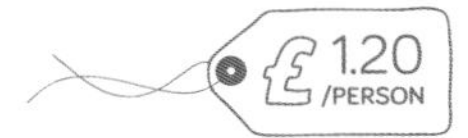

GF V

PEACH & CUSTARD BAKE

A ridiculously simple peach and vanilla custard bake. Don't forget to put a baking tray under this one in the oven: Tim thinks it looks 'fun' to have the custard dripping over it, but you should see the bottom of my oven!

1 **peach**, stoned and sliced

110g good quality **vanilla custard**

1 tablespoon **flaked almonds**

1 teaspoon **soft brown sugar**

1. Preheat the oven to 180°C fan/200°C/gas 6.
2. Place the sliced peach in the dish. Pour the custard over and then add the almonds. Sprinkle the sugar on top.
3. Put on a baking tray and bake in the oven for 25 minutes.

INDEX

Published by: Intrade (GB) Ltd
Contact: joy@noshbooks.com
ISBN: 978-0-9932609-9-5

Printed in China
1st Edition: May 2021
Author: Joy May
Recipe Development and Food Stylist: Tim May
Photographer and Designer: Ben May
Editor: Ron May
Proof-reader: Fran Maciver

RECIPE COSTS

The recipe costs in this book are an average between Tesco and Sainsbury's at the time of writing. To keep the pricing relevant, we aim to update them each time we do a new print run. Latest costs are as at October 2020.